Formative
Assessment in Action
weaving the elements together

Formative
Assessment in Action
weaving the elements together

SHIRLEY CLARKE

HODDER
EDUCATION
AN HACHETTE UK COMPANY

This book is dedicated to my beloved child, Katharine Rose, for providing the greatest ever inspiration in my quest to help children become confident, lifelong learners – and for waiting until I had finished this book before she entered my life!

Orders: please contact Bookpoint Ltd, 130 Milton Park, Abingdon, Oxon OX14 4SB. Telephone: (44) 01235 827827. Fax: (44) 01235 400454. Lines are open from 9.00 to 5.00, Monday to Saturday, with a 24-hour message answering service. You can also order through our website www.hoddereducation.co.uk.

British Library Cataloguing in Publication Data
A catalogue record for this title is available from the British Library

ISBN: 978 0 340 90782 5

First published 2005
Impression number   10 9 8 7
Year   2011

Copyright © 2005 Shirley Clarke

Cover photo © Sally Greenhill/Sally & Richard Greenhill.
Typeset by Servis Filmsetting Ltd, Stockport, Cheshire.
Printed in Great Britain for Hodder Education, part of Hachette UK,
338 Euston Road, London NW1 3BH, by MPG Books, Bodmin.

Acknowledgements

With thanks to the following local education authority (LEA) staff, schools and teachers for their invaluable contributions to this book:

The writers:

Caroline Preston-Bell, St James' C of E Infant School (Tonbridge Learning Team)

Russell Field, William Barnes Primary School (Dorset Learning Team)

Emma Goff, St James' C of E Infant School (Tonbridge Learning Team)

Laura Turner, Somerford Community Primary School (Dorset Learning Team)

Angela Craig, Fair Furlong Primary School (Bristol Learning Team)

Phil Minns, Ferndown First School (Dorset Learning Team)

Adam Parsons, St Gregory's C of E Primary School (Dorset Learning Team)

Sarah Marsh, Canford Heath First School (Dorset Learning Team)

Tim Nelson, Gateshead LEA (Gateshead Learning Team)

Teresa Bain, Dorset LEA (Dorset Learning Team)

Other contributors:

Helen Finch and Stephanie Williams, Dunton Green Primary School (Tonbridge Learning Team)

Anna Diggle, Ravensworth Terrace Primary School (Gateshead Learning Team)

White Mere Community Primary School (Gateshead Learning Team)

Roman Road Primary School (Gateshead LEA)

Carol O'Sullivan (Brighton and Hove LEA)

Alan Peat and Barry Silsby for *Thinkabouts*

All the teachers and LEA staff in the exceptional Learning Teams – this book is testament to your ground-breaking action research:

Tonbridge, Kent	Gateshead
Dorset	Bristol
Bournemouth and Poole	Portsmouth

Special thanks to:

My wonderful husband, John Holmes, for giving me Katy and for
    being my greatest admirer!
All my family, for enthusing over my work and apparently
    reading the books!
My editor, Chas Knight, for making my books so accessible and
    my life unpressured.

Shirley Clarke

Website:

www.shirleyclarke-education.org – for information about various
    courses and for updates on Learning Team findings, and to
    order Shirley's DVD **The Power of Formative Assessment**.

Contents

Introduction

1. Teachers as action researchers

Formative Assessment, otherwise known as Assessment for Learning, has now a very high profile in UK schools, featuring in – at least – the DFES Primary and Key Stage 3 Strategies, the OFSTED framework and in QCA publications. I believe that the continuing and developing interest in the subject is a consequence of its unique characteristic in the UK. Rather than being just another government initiative, formative assessment is being continually defined by teachers, as they trial various strategies, come up with their own ideas and delve deeper into certain aspects as they gain more insight. The development of formative assessment, therefore, is a result of action research undertaken by thousands of teachers in their own classrooms. This model of professional development is now respected as probably the most powerful way of affecting change, and Learning Network Communities have been set up all over the country to encourage this way of working.

I have been privileged to be part of the action research, first in various large-scale national or local projects, and now in the coordination of LEA-based 'Learning Teams'. These are spread around the country and consist of 30 teachers drawn, in pairs, from 15 schools in each project. The keenest teachers and schools are selected by the LEA and the participants make a commitment to attending all three days with me (once a term for a year) and carrying out action research in between the days. The feedback days are rich, exciting and inspirational, as teachers discuss then summarise their key findings under three headings:

> *What did you trial?*
> *What was the impact on children's learning?*
> *How did you know?*

The last question ensures a level of rigour. It means that teachers cannot simply say that a particular strategy made the children, for instance, 'more focused'. They have to say how they know they were more focused: what behaviours were manifested, what did the children do or say to make the teacher believe they were more focused? How did their work change?

The feedback is organised in phases and is then published, almost word-for-word, on my website (www.shirleyclarke-education.org). This means that teachers can find out what other teachers from different parts of the country have discovered about the same elements of formative assessment, in the same year groups. All the teams' findings are archived, so the resource continues to grow.

2. Where we are now, and the rationale for this book

When I wrote *Unlocking Formative Assessment* (2001), I was unaware of the extent to which formative assessment was a living, breathing, evolving animal. It seems to be developing so fast, I am able to write an updated book about every two years! I notice how devices which were very popular in the late 1990s (e.g. WALT and WILF for learning objectives and success criteria) are now seldom used, as teachers want more clarity and fewer gimmicks to support them. Whereas I included only minimal information on questioning, for example, in *Unlocking Formative Assessment*, this area is now so highly developed, four years later, that it is the biggest chapter in this new book, and takes up an hour and a half of my one-day courses. And yet, it is clear that we have so far only revealed the tip of the iceberg. Learning Teams are currently trialling different ways of framing questions and exploring the quality of discussion taking place between talking partners, and these findings will, I know, take our universal understanding to a still deeper level.

The title of this book is significant: *Formative Assessment in Action: weaving the elements together*. You can become very knowledgeable about the component parts of formative assessment, but still be unclear about how to weave these together through a typical lesson. Trying to fit the elements into a traditional model of teacher input followed by children's recording just won't work. This book attempts to show how the pieces interlink and overlap and often take the place of traditional input and recording. To bring this idea to life, I have sought out excellent practitioners and asked them to write up a typical lesson or series of lessons in which formative assessment is central. These pieces punctuate the book, and I have referred to them within the main body of the text. I believe these accounts will help people see that the main question here is not:

> *How can I fit it all in?*

but rather:

> *How can I reformat the lesson to capitalise on maximum learning opportunities?*

All the elements of formative assessment are, as usual, detailed, and include direct references to the findings of the learning teams.

I have also included, for the first time, accounts by headteachers of how they organised the development of formative assessment in their schools, plus two accounts by LEA advisers who very successfully enabled formative assessment to take off in the Dorset and Gateshead areas. Great things can be achieved by individual teachers, but we need risk-taking, enthusiastic leaders to really push formative assessment so that it has more global impact.

3. The content of the book

- The first chapter of this book focuses on key principles, including definitions of what formative assessment is – and what it isn't.

- The second unravels the issues surrounding learning objectives.

- Chapter 3 details success criteria – the foundation of the formative assessment dialogue between teachers and children together.

- The fourth chapter reveals new and exciting findings about effective questioning.

- The fifth chapter links self- and peer evaluation and marking. The only manageable way forward for marking appears to be to make it part of the lesson and to train children to identify improvement needs. Of course, this has more impact on the learning in any case!

■ Chapter 6 focuses on senior managers in schools and LEAs and examines their roles and key practices. This final chapter then summarises proven best ways forward – the things that really matter when embarking on formative assessment action research.

1 Defining formative assessment

> 6 If children don't learn the way we teach . . . perhaps we should teach the way they learn. 9
>
> *(Eppig, 1981)*

> 6 Every teacher who wants to practise formative assessment must reconstruct the teaching contracts so as to counteract the habits acquired by their children. 9
>
> *(Perrenoud, 1991)*

1. The history

Black and Wiliam's (1998) famous review of the literature about formative assessment established that engaging in formative assessment raises test results and equips children to be lifelong learners. A summary of their findings can be found in *Inside the Black Box*, which can be downloaded from the QCA website (www.qca.org.uk).

Formative assessment consists of four basic elements, underpinned by confidence that every child can improve and an awareness of the importance of children's high self-esteem:

- sharing learning goals
- effective questioning
- self- and peer evaluation
- effective feedback

The child is involved throughout as an active learner, with the role of the teacher shifting from controller to coordinator. Teachers often say that the biggest difference in their classrooms is in who does most of the talking. When lessons are punctuated by talking partners and self- and peer evaluation, children are actively engaged in thinking, and articulating that thinking, for much of the lesson, apart from when they are engaged in an independent task. Even then, they are encouraged to stop at regular intervals and check their work against the success criteria, or look for places to improve.

Since Black and Wiliam's clear conceptual framework was developed, formative assessment has gained a higher and higher profile. Teachers have taken the basic research principles and carried out action research, developing and defining practical strategies which have resulted in a sometimes dramatic impact on teaching and learning. Teachers often report a whole shift in understanding about children's learning, increased pupil motivation and independence.

2. Links with current thinking about learning, teaching and assessment

The following points, taken from Hall and Burke's book *Making Formative Assessment Work*, summarise the most fundamental and significant thinking about children as learners:

- *meanings and interpretations are co-constructed through discussion and activity;*

- *everyone has a contribution to make: authority for constructed knowledge does not lie solely with the teacher or in a text – it resides also with the learners, their relationship with each other and the activities they are engaged in, plus the way they are expected to view these activities;*

- *learners strive to make sense of new ideas by relating them to their prior knowledge and to the expectations that they construe, from the task or activity, about their role;*

■ *learning anything, say literacy, is about becoming someone who is able to participate successfully in that community of practitioners (e.g. readers, writers, listeners, speakers in this class, this school, etc.) and becoming someone who is able to use the tools and resources associated with that particular community of practitioners;*

■ *learning involves acquiring new ways of participating, and with those new ways come new identities for the learner.* ❜

(Hall and Burke, 2003)

We therefore need to teach children accordingly, offering them opportunities to discuss and work cooperatively. We also need to give specific feedback about specific aspects of their understanding, offering suggestions for discussion, exploration or improvement, and focusing on *how* children are learning as a means to better help them consolidate that learning. We need to train children, through extensive modelling, to be able to do this for themselves or for each other. Sadler's 'closing the gap' theory is fundamental here. Sadler established three conditions for effective feedback to take place:

❛ *The learner has to (a) possess a concept of the standard (or goal, or reference level) being aimed for, (b) compare the actual (or current) level of performance with that standard, and (c) engage in appropriate action which leads to some closure of the gap.* ❜

(Sadler, 1989)

We also need to consider whether a 'performance orientation' – use of external rewards and other performance goals, and more subtle comparative devices such as negative use of body language, tone of voice, etc, over-use of teaching assistants with certain children, sympathy over difficulty – will enable children to develop control over their learning and recognise their real achievements. In a learning culture, learning goals rather than performance goals dominate, and effort rather than ability is emphasised. *Inside the Black Box* and the work of Carol Dweck (1986) provide countless examples of the importance of a learning culture and the damage to learning caused by a performance culture.

3. Misconceptions about formative assessment

Target setting

Unfortunately, fame brings misconceptions, and they certainly abound today. Perhaps the term *Assessment for Learning* is misleading, in that it has misled some people into thinking that *any* assessment, whether summative or formative, might lead to learning, so it might as well be included. What matters is that formative assessment has had its impact because the focus has been on *deepening and furthering the learning rather than simply measuring it*. Simply finding out what children know, setting targets – curricular or otherwise – then later finding out if they met them or not, is not formative assessment. It is *the bit in-between* which involves formative assessment strategies: *how* we get the children to understand, really understand, so that they can apply skills or concepts in different contexts.

Minimalising achievement

Another misconception is that once learning objectives have been shared and success criteria have been generated, they can then simply be 'ticked off'. This is true with *closed* skills (e.g. to be able to make a list – one line for each point, bullet points, numbers or letters, etc), but with *open* skills (e.g. to create an effective characterisation) ticking off the criteria or the learning objective is meaningless. The child might have included all the ingredients yet have written a piece of limited worth. Children need to have models of quality and be encouraged to decide where success has occurred and where to improve.

4. A snapshot of formative assessment in action

Much detail and many examples of formative assessment in action follow in the rest of this book, but it might be useful to summarise, in practical terms, the kinds of activities teachers and children might engage in, which encapsulate good formative assessment practice.

1. Modelling through peer evaluation

Your initial input might be replaced by class, paired or self-analysis of one or two pieces of work generated by 'last year's class', looking at whether they met the success criteria, then most importantly, why one piece meets one aspect more successfully than the other. The class then carry out the same task themselves, perfectly equipped with models of quality and able to then self- or peer evaluate their own work effectively.

2. Success criteria

You might begin the lesson by giving out copies of a piece of work and asking the children to tell you what features they can see (e.g. in a formal letter), thus generating the success criteria for themselves, which form the basis of their focus and their evaluation.

3. Talking partners

Instead of only a few hands up, get all children to spend 30 seconds discussing a question before you take responses from pairs. All are actively involved in the learning, all are articulating their thinking.

4. Asking worthwhile questions

Instead of asking mainly recall questions (e.g. *'Who can remember. . .?'*, *'Who knows. . .?'*, etc.), plan questions which are worth asking. One powerful strategy, which works for any subject or phase, is giving a range of 'answers' for children to discuss in pairs:

> Which of these activities increase the efficiency of the heart?
> *Walking, running, golf, darts, skydiving, cycling*

We would deliberately include *walking* and *golf* to get the 'it depends' discussion going. After some basic understanding of the working of the heart has been established, this kind of discussion will actively deepen and further the learning.

5. Effective feedback and self- and peer evaluation

Pairs might first make sure they have included all the elements of their diary entry, for instance, but then work together on improving one of the success criteria in both pieces of work: *to express thoughts and feelings.* They might change one or two sentences and add some more. They look through to find places where they could include feelings. One child changes *'I got out of bed feeling sleepy'* to *'I dragged myself out of bed feeling like a grumpy bear with a sore head. I longed to stay for another ten minutes under the warm, cosy sheets.'*

5. Roles in formative assessment

Pupil perspective

From the child's point of view, the following ingredients would be an expectation in lessons:

Self- and peer evaluation	Lessons often begin with class or paired analysis of some anonymous piece of work, in which we decide whether the success criteria were met, whether it could be improved, and, if two contrasting pieces are given, which one fulfils the criteria more effectively.
	The teacher will often stop the class and ask us to check our work against the success criteria. Looking for most successful elements and making improvements are embedded in lessons. Pairs often discuss this together or swap over work.
'Talking partners'	When the teacher asks a question, she rarely waits for a few hands up, but instead gives 30 seconds or a minute for talking partners to discuss before responses are given. I know who my talking partner is and that person changes regularly. We support each other in many short, structured tasks and during peer-evaluation time when we help each other with improvement suggestions.
Being allowed to think about and articulate ideas and opinions	Talking partners means I always have to think about and articulate my ideas – I can't opt out!
Making decisions and choices	The strategies used above enable me to take a great deal of control over my learning and my possible achievement.
Feeling confident to question, challenge and seek help	Formative assessment gives me a voice, often rehearsed via talking partner discussions. I know that it is pointless to keep quiet if I am stuck at any of the success criteria. I seek help within the context of a lesson, either from my talking partner or from an adult. I know that thinking hard means I am in the process of learning.

Teacher perspective

From the teacher's point of view, most lessons are structured around the following:

Planning lessons which explore and promote learning	I make sure that the learning objective and success criteria are planned, but I know the importance of a meaningful context, challenging questions and opportunities for self- and peer evaluation for that learning to be deeply explored.
Sharing learning goals	At the beginning of a unit, I share/negotiate the coverage and find out what the children already know. We keep referring to this as individual lesson learning objectives are shared, so that children see how the coverage breaks down.
Negotiating success criteria	Although I have planned these, I use different strategies to enable children to 'own' the criteria.
Planning questions which further learning	I ask one or two recall questions, but, at the point at which the children have acquired basic understanding, I ask them challenging questions which will help them truly understand and more deeply explore concepts.
Using strategies which maximise pupil thinking and articulation	I rarely ask quick-fired, 'hands up' questions, but use talking partners constantly. Children do many short tasks in pairs.
Modelling ideas by using real examples	Instead of long periods of teacher input, I often use old pieces of work on the interactive whiteboard or overhead projector as a model for what is expected and as a vehicle for class or paired analysis against success criteria. I often compare two contrasting pieces, asking children to determine quality.

Summary

- Formative assessment is not another government initiative: it involves teachers as action researchers.

- Not *'How can I fit it all in?'*, but *'How can I restructure a whole lesson to include formative assessment, where the learning most powerfully takes place?'*

- Emphasise the fact that, given enough time, input and effort, all pupils can achieve success across the board and that ability is not a fixed idea – call them 'low achievers' not 'low ability'.

- Formative assessment consists of sharing learning goals, effective questioning, effective feedback and self- and peer evaluation.

- Formative assessment furthers and deepens learning – measuring it is not formative assessment.

- Taking on formative assessment often involves radical changes in beliefs about roles in the learning process.

INSET SUGGESTIONS

1. This chapter can be used as an introduction to formative assessment. After reading it, ask teachers to discuss:
   - how far they are already doing formative assessment;
   - where development needs to take place.
2. Teachers could report back their current practice in formative assessment in order to share successes.
3. It might be useful to ask for examples of 'measuring' so that teachers are clear about definitions of formative assessment (e.g. tests, recall questions and meeting targets are *not* formative assessment).

2 Learning objectives

> A teacher's planning should provide opportunities for both learner and teacher to obtain and use information about progress towards learning goals. It also has to be flexible to respond to initial and emerging ideas and skills. Planning should include strategies to ensure that learners understand the goals they are pursuing and the criteria that will be applied in assessing their work. How learners will receive feedback, how they will take part in assessing their learning and how they will be helped to make further progress should also be planned.

(Assessment Reform Group, 2002)

1. Balancing the curriculum

Planning the coverage of learning objectives consists of two basic elements: *(a)* the teaching of skills, concepts and knowledge, and *(b)* application of those skills, concepts and knowledge. The traditional model has been to teach first and apply later.

It is clear that we need a balance between the two types of lessons and learning objectives, in order for the isolated skills and concepts to be meaningfully placed and consolidated. It is also useful to sometimes set up applications *before* the direct teaching takes place, in order to see what children already know and can do and to build on those starting points, misconceptions or even failed attempts.

(a) Skills, concepts and knowledge learning objectives

Firstly, however, we need to look closely at the specific skill, concept and knowledge learning objectives in order to determine what works and doesn't work with formative assessment.

I have found it useful to differentiate between closed skills and open skills, because you then have clear implications for the related success criteria and whether 'improvement' is a worthwhile pursuit.

Closed skills

Some examples:

To be able to use direct speech.
To use a multiplication grid with two-digit numbers.

Closed skills are either right or wrong. You can either put the speech marks in the right place or you can't. There is a set procedure (as in most mathematical algorithms) in multiplying numbers on a multiplication grid. Closed skills are not bad – they are what they are, and many closed skills are encountered by children.

Implications for success criteria

Closed skills have easily-planned success criteria: either the steps involved or what you need to remember to do in order to achieve the learning objective. So, using direct speech is likely to include:

■ Use speech marks before and after the first and last words spoken.

■ Start new speech on a new line.

■ Start speech with a capital letter every time.

etc.

Using the multiplication grid will have success criteria something like:

■ Separate the numbers into tens and ones on the grid.

■ Multiply the numbers for the first square and put the answer in the box.

■ Do the same for the rest of the grid.

■ Total each column.

etc.

So, process success criteria are simply the elements of the learning objective, detailed. It would be difficult to teach these learning objectives without knowing the success criteria, and being unsure about them usually indicates a lack of subject knowledge.

Implications for feedback

Achievement with closed skills is about being able to do it or not. There is *no* continuum of achievement, where some children have fulfilled one of the success criteria better than others. The notion of 'success and improvement', therefore, is about seeing where you got it right and correcting any errors, or finding out what went wrong or was missed out. With closed skills, children can check their work against the criteria, and feel confident that, if all are achieved, they have fulfilled the learning objective with flying colours, as there is no possible way of improving the work.

Open skills

Some examples:

To be able to use effective adjectives.
To write a persuasive letter.

Open skills are neither right nor wrong. Children's attempts are on a continuum of achievement, with a variety of quality across the class. These are the lesson objectives which need examples and discussion about quality, using real examples as a model. What makes one persuasive sentence better than another? What makes this adjective more effective than this one?

Implications for success criteria

Success criteria (the elements of the learning objective) are often ingredient style for open skills, giving children a menu of devices which will help them, as in the effective adjectives objective, where including them all is not essential. For example:

- Use your senses.

- Paint a powerful image for the reader.

- Make sure the adjective fits the noun.

- Use the thesaurus.

- Try alliteration.

'To write a persuasive letter' is an interesting open skill, because the success criteria can be ticked off by a child as a first stage of

'success', indicating that all the necessary ingredients have been included. Possible success criteria:

- A statement of your viewpoint.

- A number of reasons for this, with evidence.

- A number of reasons from an alternative standpoint.

- Attempts at striking up empathy with the recipient.

- Recommended alternative action.

- A summary.

- Reasoning connectives.

Implications for feedback

All success criteria might have been included in the above example, but the quality of the persuasion might still be poor. This is the ideal second stage, in which quality is addressed. Either as part of the lesson, or in a follow-up lesson, children can now be shown examples of sentences which meet, say, one of the success criteria minimally, and examples which meet the same success criterion most effectively. They can be asked to discuss and analyse the differences and try to quantify quality. Now, individually or in pairs, they can look for where they best achieved against that success criterion in their own work and where they could improve. The improvements are then made within the course of the lesson, are perhaps shared with talking partners, and shared and discussed again during the plenary.

This is formative assessment in action: learning objectives and success criteria used by teachers to model the basic elements and what constitutes quality, children engaged in continual self-assessment against the criteria, working together in identifying success and making improvements.

Concept and knowledge learning objectives

Some examples:

To understand the importance of a healthy diet.
To understand the effect of exercise on the heart.
To know the key events of World War 2.

Concepts are usually long-term and need to be broken down. We might typically have three learning objectives displayed for a lesson: *(a)* the long-term overarching concept, *(b)* its broken down version for today, and *(c)* the process involved. For example, in a lesson during which children will use textbooks:

(a) To understand the importance of a healthy diet *(long term)*.
(b) To understand the impact of protein *(short term)*.
(c) To use information retrieval skills *(process skill)*.

Implications for success criteria

It is more effective to create success criteria which focus mainly around the *process* involved. So, in this example, the elements of information retrieval are most relevant, with maybe one or two success criteria about the concept. For example:

■ Decide relevant words to focus on.

■ Use the index to find these references.

■ Skim and scan.

■ Highlight key and relevant information.

■ Take notes.

■ Summarise the role of protein in the diet.

etc.

By focusing on the related process in this way, children are developing core key skills which can be applied to any concept or piece of knowledge. If the success criteria were to focus entirely around the concept, once that knowledge has been forgotten, they would be left with nothing.

Implications for feedback

The feedback would therefore focus mainly around the development of information retrieval, with some time spent on what has been found out. Success and improvement would be relevant wherever the success criteria are open, as described above under 'open skills'.

2. Sharing unit coverage throughout lessons

One of the trialling focuses for members of my learning teams has been to find ways of keeping the overall coverage of a unit of work 'up front' during individual lessons, so that children can relate today's learning objective to the big picture. Teachers sought to involve the children in the process of generating the coverage at the outset, so that they would have more ownership and therefore take more notice of it! The main devices used were flip charts, permanent wall displays, A3 cards attached to the white board for relevant lessons or fixed sheets in children's books. The coverage was written as complete learning objectives, notes, questions or diagrams such as mind maps.

Learning Team findings and strategies

Foundation Stage

Teachers tended to use a flip chart, often producing spider diagrams or clear visual images, and asked questions like *'What do you know about . . .?'*, *'What would you like to know about . . .?'* and *'How could we find out about . . .?'* The main impact was that children's enthusiasm and confidence about the topic was increased.

One Reception teacher got the children to make a poster for the coverage for reading and the same for writing for the half-term (see Figures 2.1 and 2.2), asking them what she should draw or write on the poster. She reported that the children often referred to the posters, pointing at them at relevant times and sometimes getting up to look more closely at one of the elements.

Years 1 and 2

Teachers often had permanent posters displayed showing the success criteria for elements to be covered such as instructional writing, which they found children used all the time. In fact many teachers said that during the national testing, when posters were removed, children would stare at the appropriate blank wall and appear to remember the criteria!

One teacher listed both knowledge and skills to be covered for a history and geography unit on Australia. At the end of the unit, children were asked to describe their learning as follows: *'We learned all these things about Australia and we learned this by being able to . . ..'*

Years 2 and 3

Some teachers trialled displaying all the learning objectives for a unit of work for the week ahead. Each Monday they would start with a brief introduction, then ask the children to brainstorm

Fig. 2.1 Reception reading poster

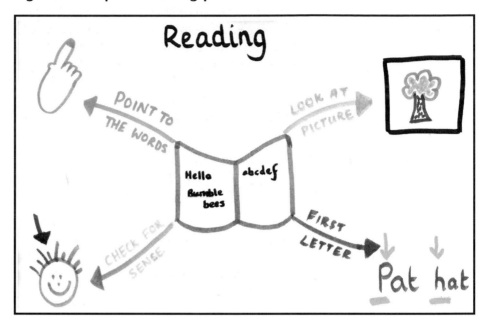

Fig. 2.2 Reception writing poster

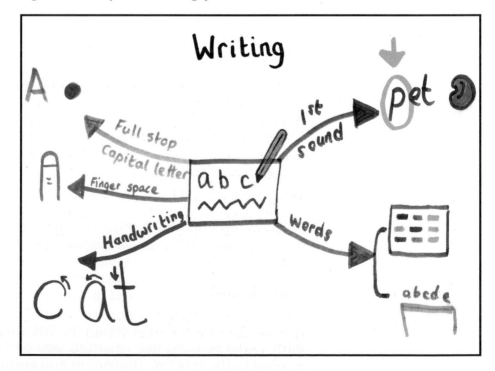

their own questions. The teachers' key questions for lessons were often drawn from this starting point. The overall impact was an increase in children's motivation and enthusiasm for the topic in hand, manifested by their bringing in *'loads of material from the internet and stuff from home'* during the week.

Fig. 2.3 shows one teacher's interesting chart of numeracy coverage for one week, devised by her and the Year 2 children on a day-by-day basis (Emma Goff, St James' C of E Infant School, Tonbridge Learning Team). She began on Monday by ascertaining their prior knowledge and writing this in black on the poster. Each day the children were asked what they now knew, and this was written up with a different colour for each day. The key objectives for the week were:

Read time to half-hour and quarter-hour (extending to 5 minutes) on analogue or 12-hour digital clocks.
Solve simple problems involving time.
Recognise relationships between second, minute, hour, day, week, and explore the comparative language associated with measuring time.

The poster enabled the children to build up and remember what they had learnt, and the teacher's main comment on the experiment was that not only were children highly motivated, but they were also seeing clear connections between the skills.

Years 4 and 5

By this age, children can refine their initial brainstorms at the beginning of a unit to questions which they think will be most useful to explore. Emma Goff, from St James' C of E Infant School in Kent, produced the science coverage sheet (Fig. 2.4) for work on life cycles. The coverage is shown as questions, skills and vocabulary are included, and children complete the final *'Other things I have learnt'*.

Year 6

Teachers reported that having the coverage permanently displayed provided a useful framework for children's ongoing self-evaluation. Constant review of the coverage enabled teachers to continually revise their ongoing plans, taking account of apparent understanding and misconceptions.

Overall, across all the age groups, teachers reported that there was more impact on children's learning and motivation if they were *involved* in the process. Motivation and enthusiasm was the most

Fig. 2.3 Numeracy coverage chart

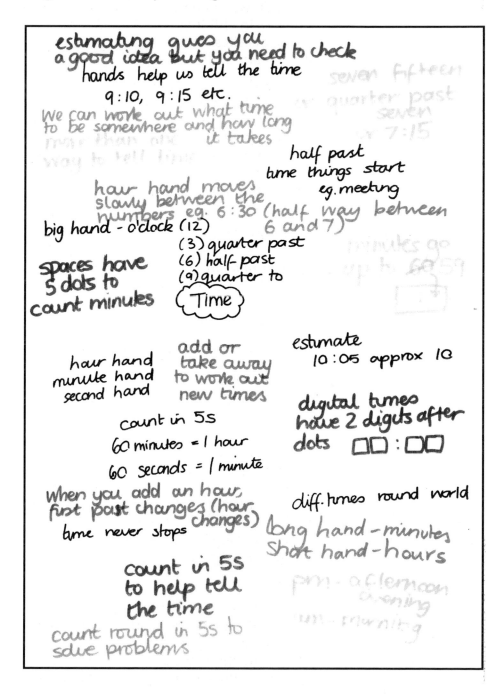

commonly reported impact. We should not be surprised that, given prior notice of what is to be covered and continual access to that coverage, children will be more 'tuned in' and motivated as lessons unfold.

Fig 2.4 Science coverage chart

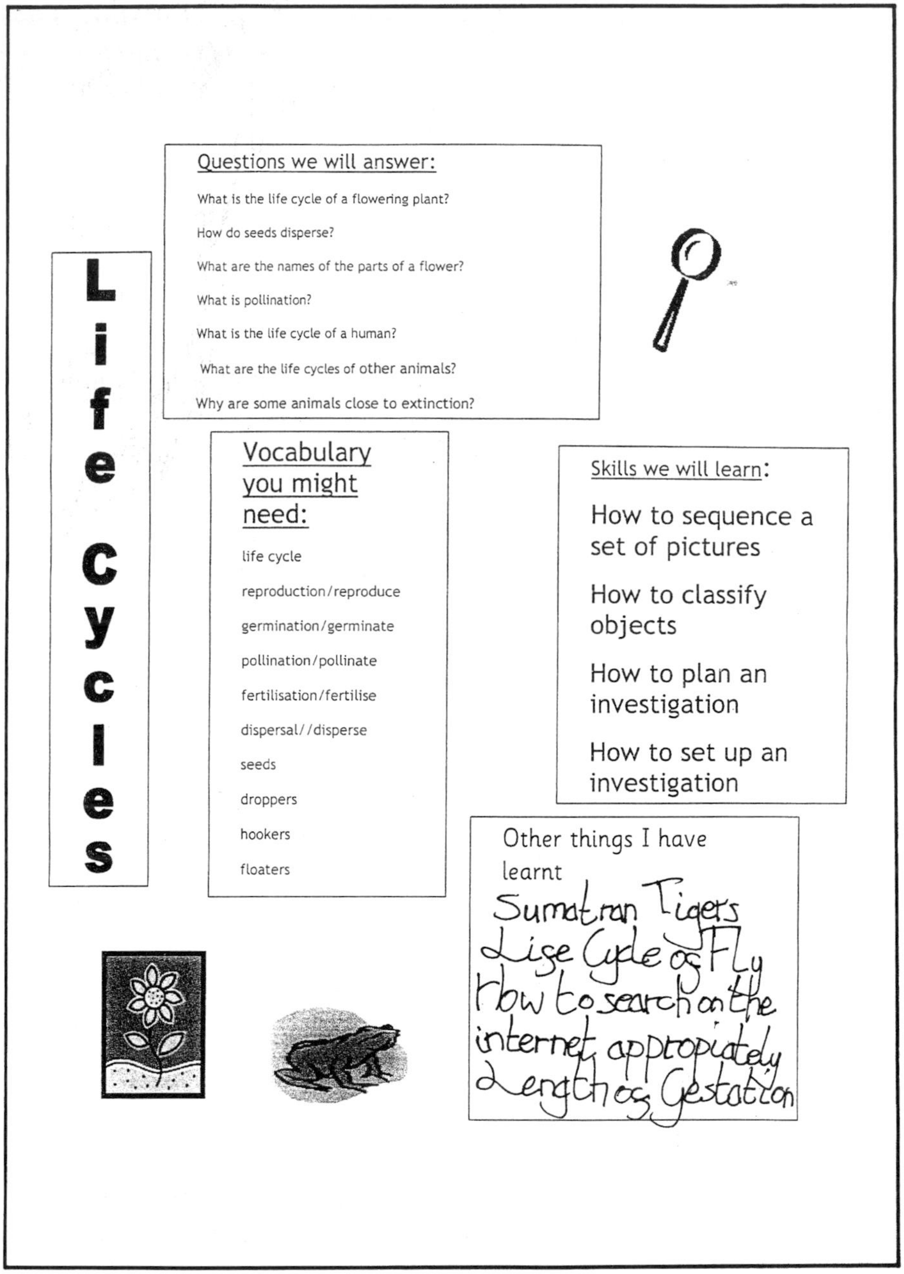

Life cycles

Questions we will answer:

What is the life cycle of a flowering plant?

How do seeds disperse?

What are the names of the parts of a flower?

What is pollination?

What is the life cycle of a human?

What are the life cycles of other animals?

Why are some animals close to extinction?

Vocabulary you might need:

life cycle

reproduction/reproduce

germination/germinate

pollination/pollinate

fertilisation/fertilise

dispersal//disperse

seeds

droppers

hookers

floaters

Skills we will learn:

How to sequence a set of pictures

How to classify objects

How to plan an investigation

How to set up an investigation

Other things I have learnt

Sumatran Tigers
Lise Cycle of Fly
How to search on the
internet appropriately
Lengths of Gestation

Caroline Preston-Bell, from St James' C of E Infant School in Tunbridge Wells in Kent, now describes how she tackled the unit coverage with a mixed Year 1/2 class around the themes of Homes, My Body, Light and Dark, and Materials. Her aim was to involve them in the coverage discussion, to find out what they already knew and to use that knowledge to lead her planning for the next two terms. As a member of the Learning Team, she was particularly interested in how to create ongoing coverage details which children could refer to as the topics were unfolding.

Weaving the elements together: Teacher Account 1

Key focus: Involving children in unit coverage

Weaving together:

- **talking partners**
- **framing effective questions**
- **children asking questions**
- **sharing success criteria**

Introduction

St James' C of E Infant School is a Foundation Stage and Key Stage One school in the heart of Tunbridge Wells. Each year group comprises 70 pupils, with single and mixed-age groupings. The focus for this study was Beech Class, a mixed Year 1 and 2 class.

The idea of a study drawing ideas *from* the children rather than the increasingly common delivering objectives *to* the children was most appealing, as I had always taught in a cross-curricular way. It seemed to echo the philosophy behind *Excellence and Enjoyment* and support the move, once again, towards greater creativity in the curriculum.

Aims

The aims behind the project, spread across four half-terms, **were to explore what happened when the class was involved in the initial planning of a unit of work** (e.g. My Body, Materials), and **to consider what impact this had on their consequent knowledge and understanding**. Clearly there would also be implications for my planning, assessment and organisation of their learning.

(continued)

The topic work

Opening up the topics to the children at the planning stage, i.e. before I had completed the customary six-week half-term planning sheet, proved to be a fascinating exercise, as was moulding the resulting framework into teachable units. However, initially a number of questions arose:

When was the best time to discuss their ideas?
How to initiate dialogue between all pupils in a large group?
How could I end up with a coherent set of objectives?
How would I ensure curriculum coverage and knowledge?
What if the children didn't have many ideas, or if these were muddled?
How would I know what they had learnt?
Did it matter if they still had misconceptions?

I decided that before introducing any more than the names of the topics (Homes, My Body, Light and Dark, and Materials) I would explain *(a)* that we were going to see what we already knew, and *(b)* that they were going to help me plan what we wanted to find out **what they wanted to know.** Using **talking partners** to encourage all to participate, the children talked to each other, then fed back answers to my questions (Fig. 2.5).

Fig. 2.5

Teacher's questions
• We are going to do a topic about our bodies. What do you want to find out? Tell your talking partner one thing you want to find out more about.

• What are materials? Discuss this with your talking partner and give me three ideas.

• What do you know about dark? What *don't* you know about it?

The results of our brainstorm were scribed onto a large sheet of plain paper and, where possible, different colours were used to group similar ideas. I tried not to allow myself to

(continued)

influence their thoughts and suggestions at this stage, for these were to become the backbone of our work over the next few weeks.

Fig. 2.6 Example of brainstorm about great-great-grandparents

We thought about how our great-great-grandparents lived.

This is what we think:

- **Their houses were built of sticks.**
- **They had mud and straw houses.**
- **They lived in villages.**
- **They had no electricity and no TV.**
- **They had to collect water from rivers and wells.**
- **They used wood for their fires.**
- **They had to walk to the shops for food every day.**
- **They had horses not cars.**

Are we right?

What do you think?

I was surprised by their current level of knowledge (e.g. *about nocturnal creatures)*, amused at their misconceptions (e.g. *that their great-great-grandparents lived in mud and straw houses)*, and interested in their reasoning (e.g. *medieval castle windows didn't have glass so that they could easily shoot arrows through them)*. Observing the children discuss the topic areas gave me a good idea about what interested them most – anything relating to **how things worked**, especially eyes, the heart; **how things are made**, like silk or glass; **why things are different**, like doing the washing in 1904. Equally I could see when their eyes glazed over or they became fidgety as I tried to enthuse about what different materials are for or labelling the parts of the body.

As the children made their suggestions I modelled how to turn them into questions for our chart. For example:

T: 'Tell me something you want to find out about the dark.'
P: 'Bats.'
T: 'What do you want to know about bats?'

(continued)

P: 'They're scary 'cos they fly at night.'
T: 'Perhaps we could write *Why do bats come out at night?*'

Fig.2.7 Examples of children's questions

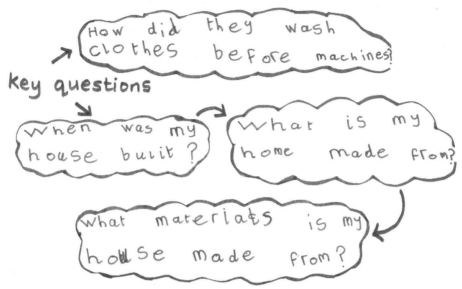

There was no shortage of suggestions for Homes, My Body and Light and Dark, but the Materials topic drew many quizzical faces. On reflection I feel this was the least child-centred topic and initially didn't seem to hold much excitement! In order to pursue Materials, I decided to create a sub-topic through which many of the concepts could be explored. I chose 'Shoes', as it was within their experience and readily resourced. We spent a day immersed in this theme following the more enthusiastic questions posed by the children (Fig. 2.8).

Fig. 2.8

Materials	Shoes
What are materials?	Why do we wear different shoes?
How are materials made?	What are different shoes used for?
How is silk made?	Are all shoes made from leather?
Why do we have materials?	Why do we have pairs of shoes?
	How are shoes made?

(continued)

Keeping a list of the questions available in the class enabled me to focus the children's attention at the beginning or during the lesson, we could see what we had found out and what might come next. As the activities developed, *Can we remember . . .?* questions were also added. By the end of the unit of work, we had not only compiled a set of objectives but also included the means of achieving them (Fig. 2.9).

Fig. 2.9

Our topic is about homes.

What is our home like?
What are other homes like?

What can we see, hear, smell, touch, taste in our homes?
Come and read our poems!

Can we label all the features on the outside of a house?
Can we remember to label clearly?

What is the process of building a house?
Can we order the steps and remember some key words?

What materials are used to build a house?
Can we see these materials on other houses near our own? (homework sheet)

Can we use 'starting graph' to record information about our houses?

How can we construct different homes from boxes, cartons, Duplo, Lego, etc?
Come and look at our models and photographs.

How did our great-great-grandparents live, and especially how did they manage to do their washing?
Can you remember what was different, what was the same?

As I was developing **a process of thinking**, it was important to use their information to demonstrate how to put together a set of questions around a subject we could genuinely explore. The danger was to praise them for their ideas but revert to the predetermined set of lessons from the school plans.

In the Homes topic outlined above, each question led to activities covering:

- **Literacy:**   poetry from first-hand experiences
          writing effective labels
          understanding a process and ordering the stages
- **Science:**   observational drawings
          using the local environment

(continued)

- **Maths**:   learning to use a handling-data IT program
- **Technology**:   designing and building with construction equipment
- **History**:   making comparisons between life now and life in the past

Using a *concept map*, I evaluated the children in order to determine what they had learnt during their topic work (Fig. 2.10). This they did not find as easy as the planning brainstorm.

Fig. 2.10

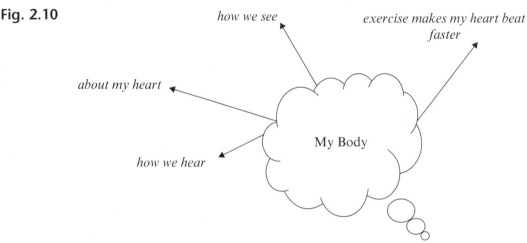

how we see

exercise makes my heart beat faster

about my heart

how we hear

My Body

I still want to find out: about hair and why blood is red.

However, their answers to *'What would you like to find out more about?'* gave insight into further areas of study, perhaps for individual study, and indicated things I might not have covered in depth. I think this aspect of the process will develop as the children experience a more enquiry-based approach to their learning. It was certainly thought-provoking: had I taught them anything?

Conclusions

- With knowledge of the six National Curriculum Key Skills,
    1. Communication
    2. Application of Number
    3. Information Technology
    4. Working with Others
    5. Improving own Learning and Performance
    6. Problem-solving

  the National Curriculum Key Thinking Skills
    1. Information processing skills
    2. Reasoning skills

(continued)

3. Enquiry skills
4. Creative skills
5. Evaluation skills

and the Programmes of Study for each subject, I was able to ensure coverage of content and skills and yet deliver a unit of work that had grown out of our discussions.

- This model of planning puts the teacher alongside the children in the questioning and learning, providing a curriculum delivered *with* rather than *to* them.
- Our discussions became as much an exercise in **how to learn** as **what we wanted to know**.
- Planning questions with the children modelled a constructive thought process where the ideas motivated the learning.
- Creative, cross-curricular links were naturally achieved, as were extended challenges for more able pupils.
- Many features of assessment for learning supported the process especially talking partners, using effective questioning (especially open-ended questions), sharing the success criteria with the children, and planning next steps from evidence of current achievement.

While many aspects of this process are not in themselves ground-breaking, the national focus on targets, curriculum coverage and individual subjects has over-shadowed the view of learning as a creative, dynamic and interactive process. Helping children **identify what they want to discover** and providing an **engaging environment** has, in my classroom, developed **motivated, high-achieving pupils with enquiring minds**.

With thanks to Caroline Preston-Bell, St James' C of E Infant School (Tonbridge Learning Team)

3. Separating learning objectives from the context of the learning

The more we learn about formative assessment, the more important it seems to be to ensure that learning objectives for lessons are *appropriate*. If learning objectives are unclear, children cannot begin to carry out the required learning effectively. Muddled learning objectives lead to mismatched activities, which may not fulfil the learning objective. They also lead to inappropriate focus and awkward or hard-to-come-up-with success criteria.

By separating the learning objective explicitly from its context, children are able to see the connections: *that learning objectives can often be applied to a number of different contexts*. Otherwise we are in danger of children believing that this particular skill or concept can only apply to the context we are working with.

The context of the learning objective is simply the activity, the vehicle for fulfilling the learning objective. It could be as simple as 'a worksheet'. Or it could be the topic chosen to best bring the learning objective to life.

Apart from making connections clear, decontextualised learning objectives make the generation of process success criteria a relatively simple task. Once you know the 'pure' learning objective, the success criteria are simply a breakdown of that objective or the ingredients which children will need to remember in order to fulfil it.

Table 2.1 gives some examples of learning objectives separated from the context.

Of course, any number of possible learning objectives might have been established from these starting points, depending on what the teacher wanted the children to learn and what stage they were at. Notice that some of the learning objectives are very specific, probably for one lesson only, whereas others might encompass a number of lessons.

Look down the middle column and imagine planning the success criteria. We need to know exactly what is involved, for instance, in creating a wash with water colours. What steps are necessary? *'To understand the ingredients of and need for a balanced diet'* is an example of a concept learning objective. The related process, comparative analysis, would form the focus of the success criteria. Exactly what would the children need to remember to do in order to carry out this analysis?

Teachers from Dunton Green Primary School in Kent, Helen Finch and Stephanie Williams, tried asking children what they thought they might learn given some unclear, contextualised learning objectives. They also asked the children what they might learn from the same learning objectives, separated from the

Table 2.1

BEFORE . . . Learning objective muddled with context	AFTER . . . Learning objective	Context
To present an argument for and against vegetarianism.	To present a written reasoned argument including 'for' and 'against' positions.	Vegetarianism.
To program instructions in the Roamer.	To program *repeat* and *pendown* functions.	Repeating patterns using the Roamer.
To ask questions about what babies need to grow.	To understand the needs of a human baby.	Interview with parent about her baby.
To produce a questionnaire about shopping patterns.	To be able to investigate the distribution of an economic activity.	Interviews with family about where they shop and how their shopping patterns have changed.
To analyse five different diets and decide what would constitute a balanced diet.	To understand the ingredients of and need for a balanced diet.	Analysing different diets.
To order numbers to 10.	To order written numerals.	Numbers to at least 10 using number cards.
To create an effective sea painting.	To use water colours to create wash effects.	The sea.

context. *The children did not know which learning objectives were which.* Examples of their responses are shown in Table 2.2. Notice how their attention is refocused on the process or key skill when the learning objective is separated from its context.

Table 2.2

BEFORE . . .		AFTER . . .	
Contextualised learning objective	What children thought they might learn	Learning objective separated from its context	What children thought they might learn
To know that household products, such as bleach, can be harmful.	'We would learn about safety and science.'	To know that chemicals can be harmful. **Context** *Everyday household products, such as bleach*	'I would be learning how to be safe and sensible and what could happen if I wasn't.'
To write instructions for making a sandwich.	'I would learn how to make a sandwich.'	To write instructions **Context** *A sandwich*	'We would be learning how to write instructions.'
To know why Samuel Pepys is important in understanding the events of the Great Fire of London.	'We would be learning about what happened and what he wrote. We would also learn how to put a fire out.'	To know how primary sources help us to find out about the past. **Context** *Great Fire of London* *Key Character –* *Samuel Pepys*	'We would learn how to find out about how other people lived.'
To be able to type a list using the return key.	'We would learn how to use the keyboard.'	To be able to use the return key. **Context** *Type a list*	'I would know how to use a keyboard and be able to find what I need to use.'

(continued)

| BEFORE . . . | | AFTER . . . | |
Contextualised learning objective	What children thought they might learn	Learning objective separated from its context	What children thought they might learn
To understand why Jesus told the story of the Good Samaritan.	'I would learn about God and learn the stories of the New Testament.'	To understand why Jesus told stories. **Context** *The Good Samaritan*	'We would learn about God and what he wants us to do and how to behave.'

With thanks to Helen Finch and Stephanie Williams (Tonbridge Learning Team)

Learning Team findings

Across all the Learning Teams, teachers found that the explicit separation of learning objectives and contexts has a positive impact on both learning and teaching:

Differentiating the context rather than the learning objective

■ Many teachers said it was empowering for lower achievers to be able to have the same learning objective as everyone else, with the differentiation taking place within the context.

For instance, the class might all be learning to use a particular mathematical procedure, but the context would allow for a range of numbers to be used. Similarly, all children might be writing a report, but some children would have higher levels of support in order to achieve this (e.g. a partially written report so that they can operate at sentence level but still have access to the same learning objective).

Planning implications

- Teachers said that they were able to be more creative with this approach, adapting the context to children's needs rather than following prescriptive content. In fact, it was common to hear that teachers were going back to the National Curriculum rather than QCA schemes of work.

- One teacher discovered that, across different sports, the same invasive skills were being used, so was able to make this clear to children by making the skill the learning objective and the context the sport.

- Foundation Stage teachers found that separating the learning objective from the context was helping them to be more selective at the planning stage, and made them focus more on how skills could be learnt rather than over-focusing on the context (e.g. one teacher had children designing Joseph's coat as a DT activity and was able to refocus the children when they got bogged down with comparing their patterns rather than their designs).

- One school decided to restructure the curriculum map by replacing it with a list for each year group of context-free objectives linked to skills that can be repeated. This was a way to bring in key skills across the whole school. They began with history, then geography and so on. They found that there are only a limited number of key skills, so you end up with less to teach but with more depth and quality. Once this had been established, the issue of progression became important, so the school is now breaking down the key skills into some kind of year group progression.

Impact on learning

- One of the key findings across the board was that children were beginning to transfer skills across the curriculum, mentioning that something had been learnt in another lesson and could be useful here. For example, adjectives were seen as useful in a science investigation, and a timeline produced for the life of Boudicca generated the following questions from a Year 4 class:
  If this was for Victorian times, would Queen Victoria be there?
  So Jesus was alive when the Romans were there?

- One school reported th[...]
from the context had c[...]
learning: they were loo[...]
something out, rather [...]
be carried out. Once sk[...]
often choose their ow[...]

- Children were becomi[...]
there was an emerging[...]
notion that children a[...]
said, 'They are able to s[...]
an overall picture of lea[...]

Summary

- Coverage needs to be balanced between skills, concepts and knowledge and applications of those elements.

- Closed and open skills usually have different types of success criteria and different feedback implications.

- To increase understanding and motivation, children need to be involved in initial unit coverage planning, and to be continually aware of how short-term learning objectives fit the big picture of whole-unit coverage.

- In planning learning objectives the context needs to be separated, in order to ensure that children fully understand the focus of their learning and are able to transfer skills across the curriculum.

- Differentiating the context and level of support is more equable and inclusive for all levels of achievement than differentiating the learning objective or the success criteria.

INSET suggestions

1. Ask staff to review the balance between skills, concepts and knowledge and applications using their existing plans. Share examples of how teachers have successfully started a lesson or series of lessons with an *application* rather than teaching.
2. Ask teachers to use short-term plans to identify examples of closed and open skills.
3. Ask staff to read the teachers' ideas for sharing unit coverage (pages 18–20) and get teachers to brainstorm any new ideas or existing strategies. In pairs, decide on one subject/one unit to trial, using only one strategy at first.
4. Show staff the section in this chapter on separating learning objectives from the context of the learning, then get them to practise, using short-term plans, planning as follows:

Learning objective/s	Context	Success criteria	Organisation, resources, etc.

5. Share examples (pairs, then fours, to whole-staff feedback) and discuss.
6. In groups, use real lesson examples to decide how differentiation could occur in the context and the level of support given. Feed back one example from each group.

3 Process success criteria

> *Communicating assessment criteria involves discussing them with learners using terms that they can understand, providing examples of how the criteria can be met in practice and engaging learners in peer and self-assessment.*

(Assessment Reform Group, 2002)

1. Defining process success criteria

Process success criteria are either a reminder of steps (as in *a mathematical procedure*) or ingredients which either must be used (as in *instructional writing*) or **could** help the child achieve the learning objective, but do not necessarily have to all be used (as in *using effective adjectives*).

Planning success criteria makes planning the activity easier, because the criteria form the essential ingredients for modelling and teaching. Once children have access to the success criteria, they have a framework for a formative dialogue, with either partners or teachers, which enable them to:

- ensure appropriate focus
- clarify understanding
- identify success
- determine difficulties
- discuss strategies for improvement
- reflect on overall progress

It is important to remember the points made on pages 14 and 15, that whether the learning objective is open or closed radically affects whether qualitative improvement can be made, or whether 'improvement' is simply a matter of correcting errors or filling in missed components.

The following pages show examples of learning objectives linked with their context, related skill where appropriate, and typical process success criteria. The language and even the ingredients could change according to the stage the children are at and the wording the children come up with.

Reception

Teachers often have pictorial representations of success criteria for younger children, although the words should still be written up. The class discussion is remembered if children have been included in the wording and the pictures, along with the modelling.

Learning objective	Context	Process success criteria
To be able to count reliably a set of random objects to 10	Buttons	Remember to: • count one by one • move each one as you count • put them in a line to check.

Year 1

Teachers often have pictorial representations of success criteria for younger children, although the words should still be written up. The class discussion is remembered if children have been included in the wording and the pictures, along with the modelling.

Learning objective	Context	Process success criteria
To be able to make a simple list.	Food and drink for the party	Remember to: • put each thing on a new line • look at our brainstorm • include food and drink • include things to hold the food and drink.

Year 2

At this stage direct speech is a long-term objective which has been broken down. Some teachers just use the illustrative examples (*'Hello Ron!'*, etc) as the success criteria, to make them more accessible. Again, meeting the closed success criteria means achievement has occurred.

Learning objective	Context	Process success criteria
To be able to use direct speech *(long term)* To use speech marks *(today)*	Harry Potter excerpts	Remember to: • put " " at beginning and end of speech: *"Hello Ron!" said Harry.* • use a capital letter at the beginning of speech: *...and Harry said, "Quick! Let's vanish!"*

Year 3

Here is an example of knowledge with a linked skill, which will form the basis of the success criteria. Depending on children's previous experiences, the success criteria are as narrow or as broad as they need to be. *'Write a summary conclusion'* could have been a linked skill on its own, with its own set of success criteria, but, for this imaginary class, they are aware of the elements of a conclusion, or the elements are displayed somewhere else in the classroom. This is an open skill, so the first stage would be making sure all the elements had been included. It would then be important to compare and discuss different quality conclusions, for instance.

Learning objective	Context	Process success criteria
To know that some materials change when heated or cooled *(long term)* To draw conclusions reflecting results *(linked skill for today)*	Find out what changes occur: *making a cake, melting and cooling, frying an egg, heating and cooling water.*	Remember to: • read your results • talk about what they show • decide what has changed or not, and why • write a summary conclusion.

Year 4

These are ingredient-style success criteria, where it may not be necessary to use them all. Again, the learning objective is an open skill, so discussions about quality and success and improvement strategies should be used.

Learning objective	Context	Process success criteria
To write an effective story start *(3 lessons)* To use effective adjectives and adverbs *(today)*	Mystery genre A series of lessons for a story start *(elements of a story start permanently displayed)*	Remember to include at least two of these: • use your senses • adverbs follow verbs • create a powerful image for the reader • look at the examples on the flipchart • make sure the adjective fits the noun.

Year 5

This is an application learning objective, as the children have probably done a lot of work on direct speech. The success criteria would be familiar to them, probably permanently displayed. As it is a closed skill, completing the success criteria correctly means full achievement.

Learning objective	Context	Process success criteria
To be able to use direct speech.	An interview with Queen Victoria.	Remember to: • put speech marks before and after the first and last words spoken • use a capital letter for the first word spoken each time • start each person's speech on a new line • use a comma before 'said'.

Year 6

This is another application, with very broad, frequently used success criteria. First stage would be to check the inclusion of the criteria, with a second stage discussion focusing on quality.

Learning objective	Context	Process success criteria
To understand the effect of exercise on the heart *(long term)* To plan and conduct a fair test	Children's own ideas	Remember to: • make a prediction • use the rules of fair testing • keep a record of your measurements • look for trends and make a hypothesis if possible • give reasons for your conclusion and link with your prediction.

Any age

This learning objective contains probably the longest list of success criteria children ever come across, with different wording for each year group. The learning objective is an application, probably a classroom test, so everything covered so far would be included. Picking one or two of the success criteria for subsequent improvement could be a follow-up, or simply treating the piece as a summative piece and giving summary feedback about the stage reached so far is also possible on an occasional basis.

Learning objective	Context	Process success criteria
To write a complete story.	Given titles	Remember to include: • an effective opening • an effective ending • effective characterisation • series of related events • use of powerful verbs, adjectives, similes and/or metaphors • check grammar, spelling, punctuation. etc

2. Other styles of success criteria

Another 'style' of success criteria can be found in *Thinkabouts*, by Alan Peat and Barry Silsby (Fig. 3.1). These are process success criteria for broad application themes in Literacy and can be found on www.alanpeat.com. I particularly like the bracketed examples.

Fig. 3.1

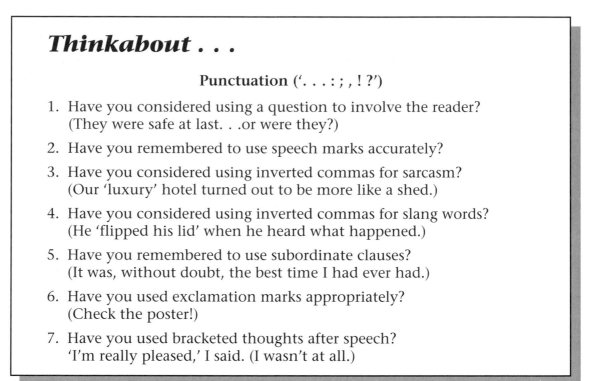

Thinkabout . . .

Punctuation ('. . . : ; , ! ?')

1. Have you considered using a question to involve the reader?
   (They were safe at last. . .or were they?)

2. Have you remembered to use speech marks accurately?

3. Have you considered using inverted commas for sarcasm?
   (Our 'luxury' hotel turned out to be more like a shed.)

4. Have you considered using inverted commas for slang words?
   (He 'flipped his lid' when he heard what happened.)

5. Have you remembered to use subordinate clauses?
   (It was, without doubt, the best time I had ever had.)

6. Have you used exclamation marks appropriately?
   (Check the poster!)

7. Have you used bracketed thoughts after speech?
   'I'm really pleased,' I said. (I wasn't at all.)

3. Generating and writing up success criteria

Learning team feedback shows that it is essential for children to be included in the generation and wording of the success criteria. There are ways in which this can be done effectively and efficiently, without spending extended time at the beginning of a lesson.

Strategies seen so far

■ If there are up to three success criteria, just before the children start to work, ask *'So what do you need to remember in order to achieve the learning objective?'* Writing the success criteria in the words the children use gives them ownership of the criteria.

■ If there are too many criteria for children to remember by the time they are ready to work (as in a mathematical calculation), write up each criterion one by one as the task is modelled, again asking for children's words each time.

■ With the whole class, look at an anonymous example of the work to be done and ask talking partners to come up with one or two features of the work. Take responses and all success criteria should be generated easily and quickly (e.g. *What has been included in this story opening/persuasive letter/formal letter/descriptive piece?*, etc).

■ Get the children to have a go at the task first, then ask them to tell you what they had to do first, next and so on (useful for mathematics calculations or any step-by-step procedure). Their answers form the success criteria.

■ For application learning objectives which recur, pre-print the success criteria and attach them to the whiteboard. Some teachers use a set of A3 laminated cards for this purpose. Frequently-used success criteria can be permanently displayed on the classroom wall.

4. One school's experience

White Mere Community Primary School, in Gateshead, produced the following account in a pamphlet for the 'Showcase' event on Day 3 of their Learning Team Project. They described the overall development of formative assessment in the school, but focused on success criteria, providing a useful example of the expertise developed by children in amending the success criteria:

At White Mere Community Primary School, we have been working with formative assessment for over three years, with support from the LEA Assessment Team.

Initially, work focused on developing learning intentions in 'child-speak' in literacy and numeracy. This was then developed into identifying success criteria and sharing them with the children. Teachers then trialled various methods of marking to success criteria (e.g. highlighting successes). This reduced work for the teacher as it focused marking on the learning intention. This then progressed to 'closing the gap', whereby a variety of marking strategies were used, including oral feedback, cloud and block (for successes and improvement), scaffolded prompts and reminder prompts (see *Enriching Feedback in the Primary School*).

Teachers and children have grown in confidence in developing success criteria. All planning now includes learning intentions and success criteria. Children can readily offer appropriate success criteria and refer to them while working as a check that they are achieving the learning intention.

Success criteria suggested by Year 4 children when presented with a subtraction question

1. Use the vertical method with counting on.
2. Check your answer – you could use the inverse
3. Keep digits in columns.
4. Write down the number you are going to next in brackets.
5. Keep your digits neat and easy to read.
6. Copy down the question properly.
7. Start with the units column.
8. Draw your answer lines with a ruler.
9. Show the number you are adding on.
10. Start by counting on to the next ten, then the next hundred.

$$
\begin{array}{r}
500 \\
-163 \\
\hline
\end{array}
$$

+   7 (to 170)
+   30 (to 200)
+300 (to 500)
_____

337

Children's suggestions needed amending, as they include success criteria applicable to various subjects (e.g. those concerning presentation, etc.)

(continued)

Amended success criteria (by teacher and children together):

1. Keep digits in columns when you are writing the calculation.
2. Start with the units column.
3. Start by counting on to the next ten and then the next hundred.
4. Show the number you are adding on.
5. Write down the number you are going to next, in brackets.
6. Check your answer – you could use the inverse.

> Zoe, on seeing these on the whiteboard, pointed at number 5, saying, *'That's where I'm going wrong!'*

With thanks to White Mere Community Primary School (Gateshead Learning Team)

The next account, written by Russell Field, a Year 5/6 teacher from William Barnes Primary School in Dorset, illustrates the effective use of success criteria for a closed learning objective. Of course, other elements of formative assessment are evident and woven into the lesson, especially ongoing peer-assessment. The teacher skilfully gets the children to identify the success criteria which are most important for them to focus on for their own progress as well as for the task in hand, and finds, through peer assessment, that many children go on to change their minds about the main targets for improvement.

Weaving the elements together: Teacher Account 2

Key focus: Peer assessment using success criteria

Weaving together:

- **talking partners**
- **self-assessment**
- **reflection of overall progress**
- **children generating success criteria**
- **peer assessment**

An example of peer assessment

Year Group	5 and 6	Background
Lesson	Word Level (incorporating Spelling, Word Level, Handwriting)	In the half-term before the lesson, the children have used regular self-assessment and daily success criteria. They have used learning and talking partners for 2 years, but not peer assessment.
Set	Top	
Activity	**Self/Peer Assessment of Handwriting**	

Time	Activity/Teaching Points/ Organisation	Effect on Teaching and Learning
Preparation	Prior to the lesson, I had taken and enlarged a photograph of a child displaying a good posture and position for writing.	
10.30	After settling, I introduced the concept of an agreed list of **success criteria** for 'perfect handwriting.' I pointed out that whilst none of us actually have perfect handwriting, it is something we should all aspire to! (All discussed within the general context of handwriting only being a part of what we call the 'juggling act' of writing.)	
10.35 – 0.45	Using **agreed learning partners**, the children listed as many different **success criteria** as possible on whiteboards. They were encouraged to use examples of their own writing, writing on the wall and a page from previous handwriting practice on the interactive whiteboard.	All children engaged. I was able to work the room, intervening where there were slight misconceptions, including a pair who were including criteria for spelling.

(continued)

Time	Activity/Teaching Points/ Organisation	Effect on Teaching and Learning
10.45 – 10.50	I asked the children to bring their whiteboards to the carpet area and we condensed their ideas into one list on the interactive whiteboard.	I was able to develop the language of handwriting during this time, insisting on the use of ascenders, descenders, etc.
	I then asked the children if there was any way we could split this lengthy list to make it more accessible. Very quickly, they saw that the behaviour could be categorised into *Body Success Criteria* (Fig. 3.2) and *Page Success Criteria* (Fig. 3.3).	All children were motivated to see aspects of their list represented in the class list.
10.50 – 11.00	Leaving the Success Criteria on the board, I then asked the children to list which of the criteria they felt were most important for *their* progress. A maximum of three, from either list.	Most children wanted to use work in their books as a prompt for their own needs.
11.00 – 11.10	Speed-writing exercise. This took the form of a dictation with varying degrees of speed constraints.	I decided to use the speed-writing exercise to replicate the 'juggling' or multi-tasking required during the act of writing. A simple handwriting/copying exercise would not have done this.
11.00 – 11.25	**Peer Assessment**. I explained that the speed writing was going to be analysed. As this was the early stages of peer assessment, I introduced the concept as 'two heads being better than one.' I felt that the very tight criteria they would be using would ensure the peer assessment would be effective.	
	Taking one script at a time, each learning partnership assessed the	The majority of partnerships were surprised to find that

(continued)

Time	Activity/Teaching Points/ Organisation	Effect on Teaching and Learning
	writing. They did this by highlighting consistently successful aspects and aspects which were consistently not meeting a particular criterion (using two different colours – a strategy they were very used to with well-practised self-assessment). I asked that, initially, they assess it against the three criteria that had been chosen by the writer. This was then extended to include all the success criteria, still displayed on the whiteboard.	what they thought were the top three issues for their writing, were not. It was pointed out by several children during this activity that they could only use the 'Page' criteria, as they had not seen the 'Body' during writing (see Development, below).
11.25 – 11.35	The children changed their 'Top 3' criteria for improvement, using the information gained from the peer assessment. These were recorded as **personal targets**, under the speed writing.	The children seemed very willing to change their 'Top 3'. I believe this to be because they owned both sets of Top 3 – the first was their opinion, the second was something they had discovered alongside peers. The final 'Top 3' therefore came loaded with ownership, and far more powerful than anything I could have advised them with, as a result of more traditional ways of marking.
11.35 – 11.45	Having prepared their targets, the children were given a chance to improve. A second speed-writing activity was undertaken. There was a brief discussion about the progress made between learning partners.	The children were used to having their Literacy Targets written on Post-it stickers so that they could be place on the page opposite their current writing. It was suggested by a child that we do the same with the handwriting targets.

(continued)

Development

1. The activity has been repeated a number of times, using the success criteria and personal handwriting targets. Peer assessment has included the following activity: **A** takes part in the speed-writing/handwriting activity whilst **B** *observes* them, looking for the success criteria from the 'Body' list (Fig. 3.2). A discussion follows, with appropriate notes for improvement.
2. Peer assessment has developed to the point where children are now regularly commenting on, editing and scribing in each others' books and work. I have found this to be most effective as part of an early intervention focus or pit-stop plenaries – where there is an immediate opportunity for an improvement to be made.
3. The development of an agreed set of rules for peer assessment. I had considered this before any activities involving peer assessment, but felt that the children needed to experience the idea in different forms before being asked to agree rules.

With thanks to Russell Field, William Barnes Primary School (Dorset Learning Team)

Fig. 3.2

B O D Y

SUCCESS CRITERIA

Writing arm on the table

Spare hand on the book

Sit up straight

Watch your writing

Fig. 3.3

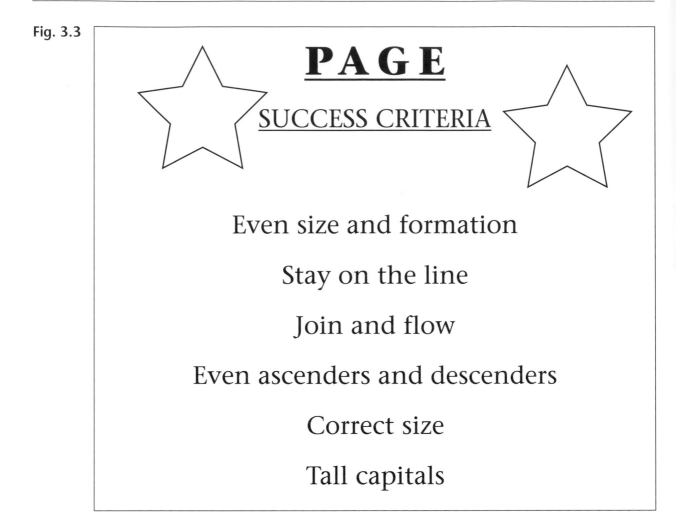

PAGE

SUCCESS CRITERIA

Even size and formation

Stay on the line

Join and flow

Even ascenders and descenders

Correct size

Tall capitals

6. The impact of process success criteria

Learning Team findings and strategies

Foundation Stage

- Mind maps© are a good vehicle for creating success criteria or asking children to come up with symbols to remind them.

- Success criteria have had a positive impact on children's behaviour.

- It is important to ask children to check the success criteria regularly.

Key Stage 1

- Children get better at generating success criteria.

- Children are more focused: they don't wander around so much.

- It is important to give everyone the same success criteria and support the task, rather than give different lists of success criteria.

- Children begin to identify a 'good piece of work'.

- Children automatically start to mark their own work against the criteria.

- It is very effective to use existing pieces of work for children to analyse.

- Less able children achieve better because they are able to access the success criteria.

Key Stage 2

- Children gradually take ownership of the criteria and therefore their learning.

- One school pastes lists of application success criteria in children's books.

- It is worthwhile highlighting the success criteria which are most important.

- It is effective to pin down one or two success criteria as a focus for improvement.

- Children with special needs are more able to work independently.

- The teacher needs secure subject knowledge to be able to know the success criteria.

- Teacher assistants are more focused on what is appropriate.

- Over two weeks, some teachers found it effective to keep long-term success criteria displayed, wiping off the specific success criteria each day.

Summary

- Success criteria are more effective if focused around processes involved in fulfilling the learning objective.

- Closed skills tend to produce step-by-step success criteria, in which all are necessary, and 'improvement' consists of correcting errors.

- Open skills tend to produce success criteria which are a menu of elements, which should help achievement and which can often be used individually, as a focus for making improvements.

- Some learning objectives produce success criteria in which all are necessary (e.g. persuasive writing), but individual open success criteria can then be used to focus on improvement (e.g. gaining empathy with the audience).

- Children need to be involved in the generation of success criteria in order to most effectively own and access them.

INSET suggestions

1. Ask staff to identify examples of open and closed skills, in pairs, using short-term plans.
2. Give pairs of teachers the learning objectives and contexts from the examples on pages 38–41 and ask them to come up with possible success criteria for these. Pairs then make fours, sharing and modifying their success criteria. Then give out the examples from the book for teachers to compare and discuss.
3. Ask teachers to brainstorm current ways of getting children involved in generating success criteria and then air any problems (usually time and difficulty in children coming up with them). Get staff to read 'Strategies seen so far' on page 43 and then discuss and decide where they might need to rethink or trial or to add their own successful strategies.

4 Effective questioning

More effort has to be spent in framing questions that are worth asking: that is, questions which explore issues that are critical to the development of children's understanding. ❜

(Black et al., 2003)

Studies about teacher questioning over the years have revealed that teachers mainly ask recall or social and managerial questions. These are, of course, the easier questions to ask, but have not challenged our children so that their understanding is furthered and deepened.

Although improving teacher questions is a continual and difficult process, it is an area of formative assessment which can result in relatively rapid, positive change in the classroom.

1. Organisation and training strategies

Wait time

Rowe (1974) found that teachers leave approximately one second before answering an unanswered question or asking someone else to answer it.

Increasing 'wait time' can be achieved by:

■ indicating the thinking time and asking for no hands up until the time is up;

■ asking for talking partner discussions for a given period of time before taking responses;

■ asking children to jot their thoughts on a whiteboard/paper for a given period of time before taking responses;

■ simply leaving more time for processing to take place.

Feedback from the Learning Teams indicates that the optimum is about five seconds' wait time, and that it is usually more productive for children to be involved in something during the wait time, rather than simply sitting up straight 'thinking'.

Extending wait time leads to the following:

- answers are longer;
- failure to respond decreases;
- responses are more confident;
- children challenge and/or improve the answers of other children;
- more alternative explanations are offered.

No hands up

Most teachers' lessons begin with an almost automatic question-and-answer recall session of the whole class (e.g. *'So what were we talking about last week? Who can remember the elements involved in . . .?'*). The typical response is that the same few children continually have their hands up and, in order to elicit the right answers, the teacher chooses the right children. If the wrong answer is given (usually children who would give the wrong answer don't have their hands up!) the teacher gives a side-stepping response and moves to someone who will give the correct answer.

Even if an open question is asked, hands shooting up all around while a child is in the process of thinking something through stops that process dead in its tracks. Many children have had this classroom experience so many times in their lives that, when a question is asked, they don't even begin the thinking process. Not only are they being interrupted in their thinking, but they are also having continual reinforcement that, compared to others, they are less able at this subject: the 'comparison effect' in action. When this happens, children gradually lose motivation and avoid investing effort in the subject, eventually opting out altogether.

Experimenting with 'no hands up' is a move towards a solution. *Anyone* can be asked to answer, which naturally raises the level of focus in the classroom. However, if the teacher continues to ask recall questions, more children are likely to be faced with the *'I don't know'* prospect. Asking a better, more open question is the aim here – but first a look at the power and impact of making 'talking partners' a constant feature of the classroom . . ..

Talking partners

Even if the question is a basic recall question *('What does a plant need to grow?')*, a more effective approach than rapid fire is to ask the question, then ask children to talk to their talking partner for say 30 seconds, to determine the answer. The answers are then gathered, with no hands up, from a number of pairs (with one child acting as spokesperson each time) until a full definition is compiled. When asking open questions *('What might be the reasons for this?')*, it is often useful to ask children to raise their hands if their *partner* had a good idea that they could tell the class.

Having 'talking partners' as a regular feature of lessons allows all children to think, to articulate and therefore to extend their learning. Shy, less confident children have a voice, and over-confident children have to learn to listen to others, so the benefits extend to a more respectful, cooperative ethos and culture: fundamental to the success of assessment for learning. We have tended to over-focus on individual children when they have responded to a question, so that the child's name is often repeated and maybe public congratulations given, thus reinforcing the comparison effect for those children who have not responded. With talking partners, the pair is asked to respond, which changes the emphasis from the *child* to the *response*.

Organising and training talking partners, regardless of their age, is essential. Some key points, derived from Learning Team findings:

- Partners need to be set and they need to change regularly so that children experience different people's ideas and personalities. Having experimented with friendship, ability, random and gender pairings, the most successful strategy across all the learning teams has been *random partners*. This was a surprise to me at first, because I imagined that children might end up with an unsuitable match, but they apparently love the fairness of this system and they know, if their partner is not of their choice, that it will change soon! Teachers from one school, on feeding back about the impact of random talking partners, expressed the view, quite passionately, that talking partners was a lot more than a questioning strategy: it was proving to be a vital, necessary life skill. They described children in their classes talking to children they would not have wanted to even sit beside in the past, listening with respect to each other's views, regardless of perceived ability, race or class.

■ The selection of random partners tends to be something like children's names on lolly sticks picked out of a tin on Friday afternoon. Those children then sit next to each other for the next, say, three weeks during lessons, the only exception being if there are ability groups for numeracy and literacy. In those lessons it is usual for children to have a different talking partner for three weeks: someone who is on their table. So a child might have three different talking partners at any time, giving them more rich opportunities for discussion with different people. When the lolly sticks for the basic pairings are picked, teachers would, of course, have to decide which pairs will sit at which tables for the following weeks, and provide a class seating plan or name on each child's new seat, or something similar, in order to avoid chaos at the beginning of the next week!

■ Even if the partners are set, it is important, at the beginning of a lesson, to quickly sweep around the room to make sure everyone knows who they will be talking to during those times ('you two, you two, you three . . .', etc). Absences mean that a number of children might be without a partner.

■ 'Magic spots' on the carpet works well for pairing young children. The mark is imaginary, but cements the child to his or her partner with limited fuss each time.

■ Some teachers have found it very successful (and great fun for the class) to model, with their Teacher Assistant or a child at the front of the class, how *not* to engage in a one-minute discussion and then, after class discussion, how to successfully work as a talking partner. Elements which you might demonstrate are shown in Table 4.1.

It can be useful to create class ground-rules from this demonstration, which are then permanently displayed in the room. Clearly, some of the important features of good talking

Table 4.1

How *not* to be a talking partner	How to be a *successful* talking partner
Avoid eye contact.	Look at your partner when they are talking.
Look bored.	Look interested.
Fidget.	Don't let other things distract you.
Interrupt all the time.	Let your partner express his or her views.
Don't listen to what they are saying.	Think about what your partner is saying.
Look as if you are listening but wait for a gap so you can say what you want to say.	Sometimes 'let go' of what you wanted to say if you think your partner's train of thought is more interesting.
Make jokes or encourage your partner to go off task.	Stay focused!
Blurt out your thoughts in a way which make you hard to understand.	Try to be clear about what you mean when you speak.
Say only one or two words.	Say more than one or two words!
Bully your partner into accepting your answer as the best one.	Be prepared to compromise or constructively persuade.

partners are skills which would need practice and training, and, for younger children, it would be useful to focus on just a few of the positives in demonstration. However, it is in looking at what is actually going on when two children are engaged in a one-minute discussion, that we can really start to plan for and develop their thinking, listening skills and communication skills: vital tools for learning.

Emma Goff, from St James' C of E Infant School in Tunbridge Wells, set up talking partners in her classroom and experimented for two terms. The success was dramatic. Here she writes up a typical mathematics lesson, in which talking partners, as in all of her lessons, are a key feature.

Weaving the elements together: Teacher Account 3

Key focus: Talking partners

Weaving together:

- **no hands up**
- **sharing success criteria**
- **self-evaluation**

- **Talking partners**
- **help seeking**

Talking partners and mathematics

Context

Children have their name on a piece of card. These are kept in a bag and drawn out randomly once a week. The children sit together with their talking partner on the carpet during each session for that week. In this lesson they are also working on the problem at their tables together.

Year 2 (mixed ability) class of 30 children, numeracy lesson focused on problem solving.

Problem

You have 15 counters and 5 paper plates. Using the digits 0–9, the counters on each line of 3 plates must add up to 10.

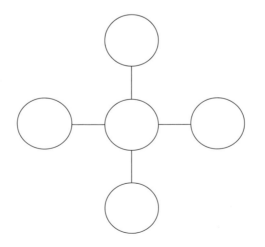

(continued)

Learning Intentions

To solve mathematical problems or puzzles.
To begin to use systematic methods to find all possibilities.
To know addition facts to 10.
To use mental strategies to add three small numbers.

Success Criteria

I can find patterns in my answers.
I can use patterns to find new answers.
I can record my work so other people can understand it.
I can check to make sure each answer is different.
I know and use number facts to 10.

Lesson Description

I began by giving an example of one way of adding three single-digit numbers to make 10. The children then had about one minute thinking time on their own to think of an alternative. During this wait time I held up a picture of a light bulb as a visual prompt. I feel that this strategy has given children responsibility to think for themselves and prepare something to say. It has also helped solve the problem of some less confident children relying on those who in the past always had their hands up first or 'switching off'. I then asked the children to turn and talk to their talking partner to share a solution. *We have invested a lot of time in our class discussing 'good talking' and 'good listening'. The children physically turn and face their partner, sitting knee-to-knee and establishing eye contact. They are also more aware of effects of non-verbal communication from models that the adults have provided.* There is a buzz in the room, and as I look around I can see children talking and actively listening to each other. Some children are using gesture to explain their solution and others are smiling back before offering their contribution. After two minutes I ask the children to turn back to me. The class are instantly smiling at me! (We have a 'no hands up' policy and smiling is our class' cue to know that we have answers ready.) I asked the children to *'Tell me one solution'* – either their own or one they have heard – and again provide a brief wait time to prepare an idea. We listed a few possibilities on the board. A colleague observing the session commented on how this appeared to 'boost confidence' and help children 'to feel proud of their achievements'.

Next I introduced the problem, explaining the rules. At this point I referred to the learning intention on a prominently displayed 'learning' board: *We are learning to find answers and patterns that solve a problem.* After providing a model example, the children went to their tables to investigate a different combination with their talking partner by manipulating counters. I explained that it was important to talk together so that we could help each other learn. The children were aware of the lesson's intentions and Miles was heard saying to his partner *'We've got to solve a problem, a BIG problem!'* and his partner responding *'but I know how to make 10 with 3 numbers'*.

(continued)

Transcription of a tape-recording of a discussion between Rachel and Jane shows their use of questioning and lines of enquiry.

R: Right, shall we look to see what the numbers make?

J: Let's see if it makes 10.

R&J: 1,2,3,4,5,6,7,8,9,10.

R: Yes, it's ok!

J: Why don't we check the top one now?

R: Or how about we do the middle one first? Look, let's make them all the same *(points to recording sheet showing a number of blank diagrams).*

J: What if we choose 5?

R: Ok, we can put 5 in there and there and there *(points to 3 different diagrams).*

J: It's always 5. Ok, now let's find the left one.

R: How about 3? Can you see that?

J: Does it work? Have we got it?

R: I think . . .. I know it's . . . 6,7,8 . . . we still need 2 more.

J: So you know that line makes 10, how about that one? *(points to vertical line).*

R: There are only 5.

J: Now, if you can just make the right number the same as the bottom one it might work, ok?

R: You don't realise it's different do you? Then there's 2 and 3 again *(pointing).* Have we done it?

J: No, we've done those before, look at the top, let's check . . . hang on . . . no, I think it's ok, we haven't.

R: We've got one more don't we? *(enthusiastically).*

J: How about we try five here instead?

R: Five at the top and in the middle. So keep zero where it is and put five at the bottom. Look, the middle number is the main number!

Using their knowledge of addition, these children trialled ideas. Through negotiating a strategy and asking tentative questions, they help clarify the process for each other. Using this system, they begin to see patterns and reflect on potential problems (e.g. starting with middle number is more effective than starting with the outside numbers). They can then (successfully) plan their next steps. The evidence could suggest that through talk the children are able to build on their ideas collaboratively, supporting each other's learning.

The lesson structure included several mini-plenaries to share such insights. This was intended to guide the children's understanding and help them make sense of the task. At each stage I asked the children to talk together to share ideas to clarify their thinking. Through verbalising their thinking it became much easier for me to assess what they were doing and how their thoughts were progressing. This process definitely seemed far more productive as a collaborative endeavour! I became aware that the children were being systematic through turn-taking: *'We did one each. Then I did the opposite of that one and*

(continued)

he did the opposite of that one. When it didn't work we put all the counters back in the middle' (Matt). The children also found patterns more easily by recognising different perspectives, for example looking at the sheet from different angles and realising that you could turn the paper to get different answers. This evidence helped me plan the next steps in the lesson, which led to frequently re-establishing the value of alternative solutions and discussing efficient recording strategies. I referred to these as *'Remember to'* prompts, displayed alongside learning intentions on the board *(e.g. remember to: count to 10 on each line, look for patterns, check that all the answers are different).*

It was interesting to notice the children taking different roles whilst talking together. James and Matthew initially agreed that *'if we need any help just say so!'* and then proceeded to assume different responsibilities.

J: 4, 5 and 5 that's 10.

M: What ones can you work out? You make them, I'll jot them down . . . That's right *(checking).* Now, what other ones?

J: Look, we could do 5 and 5 there.

M: We've got three fives.

J: Why don't we turn it now? How about this one? *(saying numbers out loud)* How about changing these 2? Is that one written down?

M: I'll look . . . .. Watch while I do it, it looks ok.

Talking together was also a particularly supportive strategy for engaging Jacob, a child with ADHD, working with Nathan.

N&J: 5,6,7,8,9,10, yes!

N: Put that one there, and this is 5. Now you try.

J: The rule is to make 10 *(moves counters).* 5 and 4 and 1 makes . . . . 4 and 1 is 5, so it's right, but look . . . this one *(points to other line)* we can't do that one, there's one extra.

N: Take it out.

J: Oh no, it's 14 now.

N: Right now *we* need to make one, you check. You helped me so I'll help you.

J: *(moves extra counter back in and counts all 15)* that's 15 . . . *(looks again and counts line)* no, that's 10.

N: We need 15 counters but there's 10 there and 10 there (pointing to lines) we need to add up 10.

J: So, *(counts again)* 9 on there, 10 on there, yes? We've done it! Let's do the next one.

Finding a solution provided him with a real sense of achievement and even inspired him to instigate the next solution.

A classroom assistant who works with the class regularly commented that she has noticed that the use of talking partners seems to have strengthened relationships, particularly

(continued)

between boys and girls. It has also given children with low self-esteem a forum where they are not so scared of getting it wrong. This was evident in Alison and Edward's work. Alison, often shy and quiet, seemed unusually confident, engaging excitedly with the task by making suggestions to her (mathematically higher attaining) partner. He was listening and acting on her ideas, adding the counters that Alison had suggested would make it work.

E: Shall we try this one?

A: We haven't got enough counters.

E: Oh, we need a zero on the end! Right, that's five in the middle and four and one on the ends.

A: And then the other five and zero. That's it!

E: Good idea, I wrote that down. What about the other way? *(indicating to swap outside numbers over)*

A: Let's turn it round. How many there?

E: 4.

A: And here?

E: This side we'll put 3.

A: And here? *(Edward models recording as Alison counts to 10)* Now turn it round again. We can do it, can't we!

To conclude the lesson the children identified *'I know . . .'* and *'I can . . .'* statements relating to success criteria. The children's comments included *'We know lots of ways to add up three numbers to get to 10'* (Emma), *'We can make a sum and keep swapping it to get 3 or 4 different answers'* (Mary), *'I know not to give up when something goes wrong, I just try again'* (Fran). I felt that the children had begun to make real progress in understanding the conceptual learning intention by identifying patterns and checking for repetition. There was significant commitment to the investigative task, shared confidence amongst the children and creative risk-taking: in Jake's words, *'We took our chances.'* They had also become more aware of the value and fun in working together, e.g. *'I can work with someone else and it's better than doing it on my own, but if you don't help each other it doesn't work as well'* (Zoë).

With thanks to Emma Goff, St James' C of E Infant School (Tonbridge Learning Team)

Other talking and listening strategies

The DfES publication, *Speaking, Listening, Learning: working with children in Key Stages 1 and 2*, downloadable from the DfES Standards website, provides a wealth of excellent material for developing talking and listening skills. It gives examples of talking partner and group activities, with specific tasks and questions for talking partners to engage in, with contexts like the organisation of role-play areas for Year 1 to pairs in Year 6 discussing the successful features of persuasive speech using Martin Luther King's *'I have a dream'* speech.

Other strategies described in the materials, which are aimed at developing *speaking*, are:

- debates – *using persuasive language;*
- glove puppets and shadow theatre – *to aid oral drafting;*
- photos and paintings – *to help construct a story or report;*
- radio broadcast: 'just a minute' – *children speak for up to a minute on a given topic, without hesitation, deviation or repetition;*
- predicaments and problems – *using opportunities from across the curriculum to focus attention on the language needed when problems are difficult to solve.*

Snowballing and envoying

The US Critical Skills Program uses Fig. 4.1 to describe the different kinds of learning styles and their related average retention rates. Teaching others is seen as the highest-order skill, the one where more deep learning occurs. *Snowballing* and *envoying* are two of many strategies for enabling children to *explain* their thinking or teach others.

Snowballing: talking partners form fours and take turns explaining their ideas to each other. Fours can then become eights, and so on.

Envoying: when children are involved in group discussion, one child from each group moves on to the next group after a given period of time. On arrival, they have one minute to summarise the key points from their previous group, and the receiving group has one minute to explain their thinking to the newcomer. This rotation occurs at set intervals.

Other useful classroom techniques for developing group discussion outlined in the DfES *Speaking, Listening, Learning* materials are:

- think–pair–share – *individual, to paired, to fours, ending in group conclusion;*

Fig. 4.1 Preferred learning styles and average retention rates
(adapted from National Training Laboratories, Bethal, Maine, 1997)

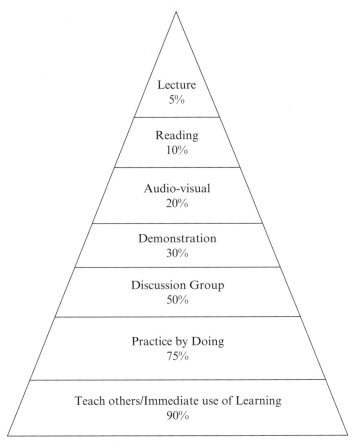

Lecture
5%

Reading
10%

Audio-visual
20%

Demonstration
30%

Discussion Group
50%

Practice by Doing
75%

Teach others/Immediate use of Learning
90%

% = average retention rates

■ Jigsaw – *children in groups receive a number 1–4; all children of the same number work together on the same research or investigation; children go back to original groups and report back from expert group;*

■ Statements game – *groups are given statement cards to discuss and categorise;*

■ Rainbowing – *like Jigsaw, but uses colours as the vehicle for comparing findings and sharing ideas after work is complete;*

■ Information gap – *groups split into two sub-groups; each sub-group is given one half of some information about a topic; sub-groups have to talk to draw the information together.*

The six 'thinking hats'

Edward De Bono's 'thinking hats' approach is an effective way of getting children to answer questions from a variety of perspectives. Children are given a question and then given a particular hat with which to think about it. This makes the thinking more manageable and more directed. The approach is particularly useful when children are involved in answering more complex questions. A visual aid of the functions of the different hats is usually displayed in the classroom, or attached to the whiteboard for lessons. Table 4.2 is taken from Carol O'Sullivan's (2003) excellent Brighton and Hove LEA publication *Questions Worth Asking*.

2. Learning Team findings about the impact of 'wait time', 'no hands up' and talking partners

Foundation Stage

- One school used Snap cards for children to find their random talking partner and emphasised the importance of changing the partners every two weeks or so.
- It was seen as most useful in training children's listening skills to get them to say what their partner said on a regular basis.
- Some problems occurred with no hands up when children wanted to go to the toilet!
- As with other year groups, it was better to get children using a whiteboard or similar as a way of avoiding 'instant recall' hands up.

Years 1, 2 and 3

- 'No hands up' led to increased confidence in mathematics, as children had more time to process their calculations.
- Talking partners gives relief from the teacher's voice and time to think.
- Children who have been used to always having their hands up and getting their voice heard first have to readjust to the fact that they are no longer the centre of the universe.

Table 4.2

Hat type	Examples
White hat thinking: involves facts, figures and information presented neutrally. This is about gathering information, so questions may include: *What information do we have? What is missing? What do we need? How do we get it?*	• What has the land been used for previously? • How many people live there? • How will the water be transported? • Will there be sufficient drainage? • Is a leisure centre really needed here?
Black hat thinking: involves caution, truth and judgement. This is about reality, identifying problems and avoiding mistakes. It promotes thinking about the validity of your line of reasoning, so questions may include: *Do the conclusions follow from the evidence? Is the claim justified? Will the plan work? What are the dangers of the plan?*	
Red hat thinking: involves of emotions, feelings, hunches and intuition, and therefore allows people to put forward feelings without having to justify them, however mixed they are! Questions may include: *What do I feel about that decision? Is my gut reaction yes or no?*	• Do I want a building in the middle this area? • Do I think this design is too modern?
Yellow hat thinking: involves looking for the positives – the sunny day thinking – advantages, benefits or savings, but they must be justified! Questions may include: *What are the benefits? Why?*	• What are the good things about having a leisure centre here?
Green hat thinking: involves creative thinking, exploration, proposals, suggestions and new ideas. It is about broadening the range of options before any one of them is pursued in detail, and does not require the logical justification of alternatives. Questions may include: *What would we ideally wish for? What alternatives are there?*	• What else could we do with the space? • What about an adventure park? • Or some futuristic green houses?
Blue hat thinking: involves metacognition – thinking about thinking. It is about reflecting on the process rather than the decisions. Questions may include: *Where are we now? What is the next step? Is this the best way to decide?*	• Was this a good way to go about making the decision?

- It is easier to see who is on or off task when children are engaged with talking partners.

- The general quality of all children's verbal responses is higher.

Years 4, 5 and 6

- Talking partners has helped improve behaviour.

- Children need to be weaned from *'well done'* no matter what their answer, to *'thank you'* when the teacher is gathering responses.

- Snowballing is fantastic for mathematics (pairs, go to fours, then eights).

- The verbal contributions of girls has increased considerably.

Quotes from children about talking partners from Anna's class at Ravensworth Terrace Primary School, Gateshead

'*I think talking partners is good because if you talk together it gives more ideas and helps us a lot.*'

'*Every Friday we change partners. I enjoy changing partners because it helps me and I get to mix with other people. I really enjoy changing partners.*'

'*What I like about talking partners is that you learn to get along with people who you're not really friendly with. I like the surprise of who you're sitting next to.*'

'*We have our names on lolly sticks and Miss picks one out. That person has to stay where they are and the second person she picks out has to go and sit next to that person. I really enjoy changing partners because you can talk to them and help them if they are stuck.*'

'*Talking partners helps me a lot because people who I talk to help me to understand things.*'

'*Our talking partners help us to discuss our ideas with other people and see which idea is better.*'

'*I think partners are a good idea because sitting next to one person for a whole year is boring.*'

3. Framing the question

Perhaps the hardest skill is thinking up truly effective questions – questions which will allow children to challenge their thinking and further and deepen their understanding. Instead of moving on to new coverage once we believe children have basic understanding, it seems that this is the very point where we should be asking questions which will get them really thinking, thus *deepening* their understanding to a level which is more likely to ensure that it is not only consolidated, but can then be used in a variety of contexts.

I have sought out, from teachers, examples of good strategies for framing questions, which can be applied to any subject and any age group. Having discovered five excellent ways of reframing recall questions, these strategies are outlined now and have begun to be trialled by the Learning Teams. From the experience of my one-day courses, teachers need to practise answering these questions for themselves (with their talking partner, of course) then have a go at changing a recall question from their short-term plan into a better question, using one of the strategies. As with all formative assessment, the importance of taking one thing at a time is vital – having a go at one questioning strategy across the different subjects until you have a feel for what works and what doesn't. Of course, as these five strategies are trialled, new excellent questioning strategies will, inevitably, emerge.

Strategy 1: Giving a range of 'answers'

From initial Learning Team findings, it seems that that easiest strategy to begin with is changing recall questions into questions with a range of possible 'answers', giving those answers (written on the whiteboard) to the children to discuss with their talking partners, then taking responses. *Note that all of these questioning strategies are intended to be used once children have basic understanding.*

With this strategy, children need to decide which are the right answers . . . which are close answers, and why . . . which answers can't be right, but how they might have been arrived at . . . or which answers can't be right, and why. This strategy has the potential for rich and fruitful follow-up exploration. Some examples . . .

Table 4.3

Original, limited 'recall' question	Question reframed by giving it with a range of answers to discuss
What is 5 squared?	*Discuss these 'answers'. Give possible reasons for the wrong ones: 3, 7, 10, 25, 125*
Which physical activities improve the efficiency of the heart?	*Cycling, walking, golf, swimming, skydiving, darts*
What makes a good friend?	*Kindness, always honest, shares their sweets, a bully, someone good looking, someone loyal*
What does a plant need to grow?	*Air, water, lemonade, light, heat, sand, soil, milk*

Planning the 'answers' consists of thinking of, say, two things which are *definitely right answers*, two which are clearly *wrong* and two which will promote discussion, the kind of *'it depends'* answers. In the second example, for instance, *cycling* and *swimming* have been planted as the definites, *darts* and *skydiving* as the definitely nots and *walking* and *golf* as the 'it depends'.

Trying these out in the staff room produces great debate and discussion, and sometimes your initial thoughts are challenged, as someone points out an *'it depends'* for an *'answer'* you thought was a definite! One of my one-day course audience tasks is to get teachers to come up with a list of possible answers to this question:

Why did Hitler want Arian supremacy?

For the definite answers, people often give suggestions which other teachers dispute, such as:

> *'He was mad.'*
> *'He wanted personal power.'*
> *'Fear of other races.'*

so these have to then go into the *'it depends'* category.

We usually get to a consensus on this kind of statement:

> *'He believed Germany would be a better place without other races.'*
> *'He believed that Arians were the master race.'*

Typical 'wrong answers' teachers suggest are:

> *'He preferred blondes.'*
> *'His star sign was Aries.'*

There is always a wealth of *'it depends'* suggestions, such as:

> *'He had an inferiority complex.'*
> *'He was jealous of the Jews.'*
> *'He wanted personal power and fame.'*
> *'He was mad.'*
> *'He wanted to create more space in the country.'*

Learning Team findings for this strategy

Foundation Stage and Key Stage 1

- Very effective: responses were more sophisticated because children had to give their reasons.

- You have to remember that children need basic understanding of the subject matter for this to work.

- Some people started by giving children four cartoon answers and children had to discuss which one was right.

Key Stage 2

- Children begin to use language like *'I'd like to challenge that'* or *'I've changed my mind'*.

- It forces you to get away from recall questions: this has changed the classroom ethos and the 'range of answers' strategy produces the most interesting talk.

- One head said that, after visiting a classroom where this strategy was really working, he felt for the first time that he was lagging behind and had a lot to learn.

- You find that you set it all up but then you can step back and let the children's discussion take over.

- You need to make sure you have the subject knowledge too – some Year 6 children know a lot!

Strategy 2: Turning the question into a statement, for children to agree or disagree with, giving reasons

The next most popular questioning strategy so far is taking a recall question and turning it into a statement for children to discuss with their talking partner. You can see that this is of a higher order than the 'range of answers' strategy, because children have to come up with their own examples to illustrate their views. Feedback from one school:

> *When given a statement to reflect upon, children truly want to defend and explain their view – and often, as they have become good listeners, are open to change their view through discussion. This strategy fosters high quality child-to-child discussion and feedback to the class.*

Table 4.4 gives some examples.

Table 4.4

Original, limited 'recall' question	Question reframed by turning it into a statement for children to agree with, disagree with and say why
Which forms of exercise improve the efficiency of the heart?	*All forms of exercise improve the efficiency of the heart. Do you agree or disagree, and why?*
Which metals are magnetic? Which are not?	*All metals are magnetic. Do you agree or disagree, and why?*
When is friction useful? Not?	*Friction is always useful. Do you agree or disagree, and why?*
Which colour cars go fastest?	*Red cars go fastest. Do you agree or disagree, and why?*
Why did Goldilocks go into the three bears' cottage?	*Goldilocks was a burglar. Do you agree or disagree, and why?*
Which drugs are bad for you?	*All drugs are bad for you. Do you agree or disagree, and why?*
What did people think of Jesus?	*Everyone Jesus met was pleased to see him. Do you agree or disagree, and why?*
Why do we need prisons?	*We need to have prisons. Do you agree or disagree, and why?*

Strategy 3: Finding opposites, or one that works and one that doesn't, and asking for reasons

The next questioning strategy is to, again, take a limited recall question, think of an example for that theme which is right and one which is wrong, show these to the children and ask them to decide why one is right and why the other is wrong. So far, teachers have given positive feedback about the value of using this strategy for mathematics (wrong and right sums) and spelling, grammar and punctuation (correct and incorrect examples). Being presented with right and wrong answers appears to give children more prompts, modelling and opportunity for thinking and discussion than simply being asked to work something out from scratch. Remember that all of these strategies are being trialled with talking partners, rather than as whole-class, 'hands-up' questions.

Table 4.5 shows some examples of this strategy.

Table 4.5

Original, limited 'recall' question	Reframed question, showing examples of opposites
What makes a healthy meal?	*Why is this a healthy meal and this an unhealthy meal? (given pictures or real examples.)*
What do plants need to grow?	*Why is this plant healthy and this plant dying?*
What do we need to make a circuit work?	*Why does this circuit work and this one not?*
What makes a ball bounce?	*Why does this ball bounce and this one doesn't?*
How do you do this sum?	*Why is this sum right and this sum wrong?*
Who can grammatically correct this sentence?	*Why is this sentence grammatically correct and this one not?*

Strategy 4: Giving the 'answer' and asking how it was arrived at

Another way of transforming recall questions is to go straight to the answer and ask children to explain it.

Table 4.6 shows some examples.

Table 4.6

Original, limited 'recall' question	Reframed question, giving the 'answer' first
Can you name some connectives?	*Why do we use the word 'connectives' for words like 'but' and 'so'?*
What do we need for an effective description?	*Why is this an effective description?*
What are the properties of plastic?	*Why is plastic a good material for modern toys?*
Can you give me an example of a complex sentence?	*This is a complex sentence – why?*
What are the properties of paper, card and wood?	*Paper is a good material for tissues – why?*
7+3+2 = ?	*7+3+2 = 12. What strategies did you use to come up with the answer?*

Strategy 5: Asking a question from an opposing standpoint

Finally, asking a question from an opposing standpoint can be challenging for teachers and children. There is the potential to discuss controversial issues in depth, so it is up to the teacher to decide what subjects will be acceptable. This is a very effective strategy for discussing Personal, Social & Health Education issues. Notice in the examples in Table 4.7 that the original questions are actually good questions, but follow expected and conventional thinking. The reframed questions force children to think of issues from an unconventional standpoint.

Table 4.7

Original question	Reframed question, taking an alternative stance
Why is it wrong to steal?	*What would a mother whose children were starving think about shoplifting?*
What are the hazards of smoking?	*Should smoking be a matter of choice?*
Why is it good to recycle?	*Why would a plastics manufacturer promote recycling?*
How did Goldilocks feel when she saw the three bears' cottage?	*How did the three bears feel upon discovering Goldilocks in their house?*
Why was it cruel to employ Victorian children to clean chimneys?	*How would Victorian industrialists justify their employment of children?*

Bloom's Taxonomy

Bloom identified a hierarchy of questions that are extremely useful for helping teachers to move classroom questions beyond the literal, and to support differentiation within the classroom. The examples of Bloom's questions 'brought to life' are taken from the Brighton and Hove LEA publication *Questions Worth Asking* (Table 4.8) and the Kent publication *Open Questions to Develop Thinking across the Foundation Stage and Key Stage 1 curriculum* (Table 4.9). The Kent examples powerfully illustrate the differences between the different types of questions, enabling teachers to more easily apply them to their own classroom contexts.

Table 4.8 Examples from *Questions Worth Asking*

	What children need to do	Examples of possible question structures
Knowledge	Define, recall, describe, label, identify, match, name, state	*What is it called?* *Where does . . . come from?* *When did it happen? Who?* *What types of triangles are there?*

(continued)

Table 4.8 (continued)

	What children need to do	Examples of possible question structures
Comprehension	Translate, predict, explain, summarise, describe, compare (events and objects), classify	*Why does he . . .?* *Explain what is happening in the crater . . ..* *So how is Tim feeling at this point?* *What are the key features . . .?*
Application	Demonstrate how, solve, try it in a new context, use, interpret, relate, apply ideas	*What do you think will happen next?* *Why?* *So which tool would be best for this?* *Put the information into a graph.* *Can you use what you now know to solve this problem . . ..*
Analysis	Analyse, explain, infer, break down, prioritise, reason logically, reason critically, draw conclusions	*What patterns can you see in the way these verbs change?* *Why did the Germans invade?* *What assumptions are being made . . .?* *What is the function of . . .?*
Synthesis	Design, create, compose, combine, reorganise, reflect, predict, speculate, hypothesise, summarise	*Compose a phrase of your own using a syncopated rhythm.* *What is the writer's main point?* *What ways could you test that theory?* *What conclusions can you draw?*
Evaluation	Assess, judge, compare/ contrast, evaluate	*Which slogan is likely to have the greatest impact?* *Should they develop the green-field or the brown-field site?* *Which was the better strategy to use?*

Table 4.9 Examples from *Open Questions*

Stories		*Each Peach Pear Plum*
Thinking process	**What it means**	**Sample questions and tasks**
Knowledge	To recall information received	• *Where was Tom Thumb hiding?* • *What is a cellar?*
Understanding	To show understanding of information by summarising or reinstating in own words.	• *Why were the bears out hunting?*
Application	To use previously learned information in a new situation.	• *Where do you think the Wicked Witch lives?* • *What do you think Cinderella is going to dust?*
Analysis	To develop skills of inference and deduction	• *How do you think the three bears felt when they saw Baby Bunting in the river?*
Synthesis/ Speculation	To formulate a new theory, argument or summary based on informed understanding.	• *What do you think happened next (i.e. when everyone saw the plum pie)?*
Evaluation	To judge the value of ideas or materials and articulate reasons.	• *How can we change the rhyme?* • *How does the new rhyme change the story?*

Open Questions also provides examples of Bloom questions for nursery rhymes, non-fiction and all the areas of the curriculum. In Table 4.10 I have taken just the final column of the six types of questions in order to show three excellent examples from the book.

Table 4.10 More examples from *Questions Worth Asking*

	Non-fiction: *The Clothes Shop*	DT: Paper and glue	Art: *The Pond*, by L. S. Lowry
Knowledge	What would you buy in a clothes shop? Who will you see in the shop? How are the clothes stored?	Tell us about your picture/model How did you begin your picture/model?	Who painted the picture? What can you see in the picture? How many houses can you count?
Comprehension	What is a till? Why are clothes different sizes?	How did you decide on your picture/model? Who is your picture for?	What is a chimney? What is a pond? Is this the town or the country?
Application	What do you need to take with you when you go shopping? How can you pay for your shopping?	Which glue did you use for the tissue/shiny paper? Did you use different glue for the coloured card? Why?	What makes you think it is town/country? Where do you think the people are going? What time of day do you think it is? Why is smoke coming out of the chimneys?
Analysis	Why do you need to buy new clothes?	What happens when you put one colour tissue paper over a different colour?	What do you think the artist was thinking as he painted?

(continued)

Table 4.10 (continued)

	Non-fiction: *The Clothes Shop*	DT: Paper and glue	Art: *The Pond*, by L. S. Lowry
Analysis *(cont.)*	How are the clothes made and delivered to the shop? What would happen if the shop sold out of clothes?	What happens if you put coloured cellophane over coloured tissue?	How does the painting make you feel? Why do you say that? How do you think the people in the picture are feeling? Why?
Synthesis	If you had a shop what would you sell? What sort of bag would you give your customer to carry the shopping home in?	What else could you add to make it sparkly/shiny/ bright? Are there any other ways you could change the colours? Are you pleased with your picture/model?	How could you make it a brighter day? Could you paint different types of houses?
Evaluation	What makes a good shop?	Are you pleased with your picture/model? Would you do anything different next time?	What would be different in your painting? Why do you think this would be better?

Encouraging children to generate their own questions

When children are involved in developing their own questioning skills, they are actively involved in their own learning. The findings from the Suffolk LEA (www.slamnet.org.uk) action research project indicated that children were:

- developing independence;

- taking more responsibility for their own learning;

- working through difficulties rather than asking for help;

- able to explain and express themselves more easily;

- thinking about what they were trying to achieve by asking questions;

- seeking explanations and alternatives more frequently;

- starting to manipulate their learning;

- reflecting on/evaluating their own understanding and often taking it further.

The following examples of working in role are given in the DfES *Speaking, Listening, Learning* materials. These are useful classroom techniques to engage children in not only asking questions, but also in developing speaking and listening skills in motivating contexts:

- Freeze frames – *still images or silent tableaux representing characters at a given moment;*

- Thought tracking – *children speak the thoughts of one of the characters;*

- Conscience alley – *children form two lines, each voicing opposing views of the character's thoughts;*

- Forum theatre – *an incident or event is seen from different points of view;*

- Meetings – *teacher in role holds a meeting leading to a group discussion;*

- Hot seating – *class asks questions of someone in role as a character;*

- Paired improvisation – *pairs in role improvise dialogue;*

- Flashbacks and flash forwards – *children focus on the consequences of action rather than the action itself.*

Excerpt from *Assessment for Learning* (Black *et al.*, 2003)

The children were eventually going to engage in a piece of autobiographical writing. The lesson entails giving a Year 7 mixed-ability class a brief passage called 'The Sick Boy', which the teacher had adapted from Laurie Lee's novel *Cider with Rosie*, so that it was devoid of detail of any kind, giving the barest outline of events with little attention to the vocabulary or, to use the technical term, lexical density. The children were asked to annotate the text with any questions they would like to put to the author to make the text more interesting. The ideas were shared with partners as the teacher went around the class listening to the questions and prompting children to think of further ideas.

The questions were then collected and discussed by the class as a whole. The class were then read the actual extract from Laurie Lee's book and the children were asked to see how many of the questions were answered in the original text. This too was discussed. The lesson ended and was followed by another lesson immediately after lunch in which the questions were categorised as **factual**, such as *'What was someone's name?'*, or as **reactional empathetic**, such as *'How did this make the mother feel?'* Lee's passage answered both types of question. These types of question were then used as the basis for the criteria by which the children' work was to be assessed. In other words, the teacher made explicit, as they began to write, that the features they had identified as helping to make the piece of writing more interesting would be the features by which their own work would be judged.

Teachers on my courses have also suggested:

■ interviews *(each other, visitors)*;

■ feely bags;

■ a stimulus start such as a picture, a piece of music, an artefact, etc;

■ creating topic or test questions for each other or the teacher (needs discussion and analysis).

The following description of a teacher asking children to develop their own questions illustrates a number of other strategies in action: sharing success criteria, talking partners, teacher prompting and modelling. Children are actively involved in formative assessment processes. The lessons show how formative assessment informs planning: the children's understanding is clearly revealed, giving pointers for future lessons.

4. The role of the teacher in creating a supportive climate

When children get an answer wrong, or it is not the answer the teacher wanted to hear, it is important to avoid 'put downs' – either by tone of voice or words used. When challenging questions are asked, it is useful to make children aware of what you are expecting: *'I expect this to be a question many of you will have to really think about. I'm not expecting right answers, just your thoughts at this moment. Say anything and we'll see what we can pool together.'*

Some effective ways of responding to wrong and right answers to encourage more thinking and less reliance on the teacher include:

■ **Gathering**: *'Thank you. Does anyone have a different idea/answer/agree/disagree/have something to add?'* until a collective agreement is reached.

■ **Asking for explanation of wrong answers so that incorrect answers are used to advantage – for example**:

Teacher: *Is this apple dead or alive?*
Child 1: *Dead*
Teacher: *Why do you think it's dead?*
Child 1: *When it was on the tree it was part of the living tree, but it's not now.*
Teacher: *Who agrees? Is there anyone who disagrees?*
Child 2: *We don't know that it's dead . . . a bit could still be alive.*
Child 3: *I think that's possible, because if you put the pips in the ground they'd grow . . ..*

(from *How do they walk on hot sand?* Suffolk LEA, 2002)

■ **Echo**: *'Seventeen.' 'Who would like to agree? Who would like to disagree?'*

■ **Stalling**: *'Hold that thought. Let's carry on and then come back to that later'*, giving a chance for the child to self-correct after more discussion has illuminated things.

■ **No pressure**: *'So what might the answer have been? Say anything you like.'*

■ **Transfer**: *'You must be a mind reader. That was the answer to another question I was going to ask!'*

- **Invite children to elaborate**: *'Would you say a little bit more about that.' 'I am not sure I'm certain I know what you mean by that.'*

- **Make a suggestion**: *'You could try . . ..'*

- **Offer extra information**: *'It might be useful to know also that . . .' 'I think that I have read that . . ..'*

- **Reflect on the topic**: *'Perhaps we now have a way of tackling this next time you . . .' 'Let's bring this altogether . . ..'*

We need to aim for a supportive ethos where even wrong answers are seen as useful (if they are followed by discussion and exploration) and children can say *'pass'* to a question without fear of failure. However, our classroom traditions have for many years encouraged children to feel demoralised about their abilities, so the supportive climate needs to be carefully developed.

Summary

- Children need approximately five seconds' wait time, best with some structure (e.g. whiteboards or talking partners).

- 'No hands up' increases wait time and child focus, but used with recall questions is counter-productive.

- Having talking partners/groups before responding to questions enables all children to participate, think and articulate and develop life skills of social interaction.

- Talking partners need to change regularly in order for children to have varying experiences – *random* pairings are most effective.

- Encouraging children to develop their own question furthers their independence as learners.

- Effective questioning involves effective modelling.

- Effective questions should further and deepen learning rather than simply help establish prior knowledge.

- Teachers need to create a supportive climate so that 'put downs' are avoided and children can articulate their ideas without fear of failure.

INSET suggestions

1. Present the whole chapter to staff and discuss perceived strengths and needs in existing practice. Focus particularly on recall questions and their usefulness.
2. Get teachers to introduce talking partners, asking them to model 'good' talking partners and 'bad' talking partners with a child or teaching assistant first. Feed back findings after two or three weeks. Where talking partners already exist, teachers can decide any modifications to trial mentioned in the chapter.
3. Plan together some good questions for one lesson, based on one or more of the strategies for framing questions given on pages 68–75. Work on these planned questions together before using them in the lessons. Use them with one or two minutes' talking partners each time and report back findings.
4. Continue trialling, building up different elements and techniques from the chapter.

5 Self- and peer evaluation, feedback and marking

> Independent learners have the ability to seek out and gain new skills, new knowledge and new understandings. They are able to engage in self-reflection and to identify the next steps in their learning. Teachers should equip learners with the desire and the capacity to take charge of their learning through developing the skills of self-assessment.
>
> *(Assessment Reform Group, 2002)*

Self- and peer evaluation and feedback, including marking, have been combined in this chapter in order to show how closely and necessarily they are woven together. Children involved in peer assessment, for instance, are giving feedback to each other; paired marking *is* peer evaluation; teacher marking *is* feedback. By separating them into two chapters, it could look as if children should be given opportunities for self- and peer evaluation as a separate activity from giving feedback to each other, or receiving feedback from the teacher.

With the exception of occasional work marked away from the children, the idea is that these elements should be woven together and form part of the fabric of a lesson or series of lessons. Marking away from children has less value than we previously thought, although traditions tend to continue even though people know their efforts are having little impact. *The new emphasis on feedback in this chapter is around extensive modelling and training during lessons, so that children are empowered to 'mark' their own work and work together on improvements during lessons.*

1. The impact of traditional feedback on children's motivation and achievement

Whether feedback is oral or written, there are some key features which can be drawn from a great deal of classroom research.

When the Black and Wiliam (1998) review of formative assessment was published, the aspect which received most media attention was their findings about teachers' feedback to children. The traditional forms of feedback have, at worst, led to regression in children's progress and, commonly, have little or no impact. Key negative elements are the giving of grades for *every* piece of work, and external rewards such as stickers and merit marks given for individual pieces of work (not to be confused with attainment awards, such as swimming certificates, which, over time, anyone can attain – see Chapter 1). Also loaded with potential to reinforce for children a sense of failure and lack of ability are: the teacher's tone of voice; body language; how difficulty with learning is talked about; the over-use of teaching assistants with certain children; and the words used by teachers when interacting with children.

Ruth Butler (1988) carried out a controlled experimental study in which she set up three ways of giving feedback to three different groups of same age/ability children:

- marks or grade
- comments
- marks or grades *and* comments (the most common approach by UK secondary teachers).

The study showed that learning gains (measured by exam results) were greater for the 'comment only' group, with the other two groups showing no gains. Where even positive comments accompanied grades, interviews with children revealed that they believed the teacher was 'being kind' and that the grade was the real indicator of the quality of their work.

On the whole, feedback has been a mainly negative experience for most children. Token comments at the bottom of work praising effort do not fool children, because the grades or rewards, and spelling and grammar corrections, tell children the 'truth' about their work.

Even 'comment only' feedback has less impact on children's progress than children being actively involved in self- and peer assessment against success criteria and, through continual modelling, identification of successes and on-the-spot improvement made during lessons.

2. What we now know about effective feedback (from teachers or from children to each other)

(a) Focus feedback on the learning objective/success criteria of the task

Teachers have, in the past, apparently focused their oral or written feedback on four main elements: presentation, quantity, surface features of any writing (especially spelling) and effort. Most school assessment policies also draw significant attention to these four main elements, which reinforces this practice. While these aspects are important, we have *over*-emphasised them, so that the main focus of the lesson has been marginalised. What you put in is what you get out, so the message to children has been clear: get these things right and you will do better.

Effective feedback involves being explicit about success criteria. The other four features should be attended to every now and again rather than at every stage, and this needs to be reflected in any whole-school assessment policy.

(b) Aim to close the gap

Sadler (1989) established three conditions for effective feedback to take place:

> *The learner has to (a) possess a concept of the standard (or goal, or reference level) being aimed for, (b) compare the actual (or current) level of performance with the standard, and (c) engage in appropriate action which leads to some closure of the gap.*

Improvement suggestions, therefore, need to be focused on how best to close the gap between current performance and desired performance, specific to the learning objectives in hand.

(c) Give specific improvement suggestions

Kluger and DeNisi's (1996) research review showed that feedback only leads to learning gains *when it includes guidance about how to improve*. Terry Crooks (2001), as a result of his review of literature about feedback and the link with child motivation, concluded that:

the greatest motivational benefits will come from focusing feedback on:

- *the qualities of the child's work, and not on comparison with other children;*

- *specific ways in which the child's work could be improved;*

- *improvements that the child has made compared to his or her earlier work.*

Specific and *improved* are two key words in Crook's recommendations. We have tended to be too general in the past to be helpful to children (e.g. *'some good words here'* or broad targets such as *'remember to include more detail in your prediction'*). We have also tended to focus feedback on *correction* rather than *improvement*.

It is often the case that, instead of giving specific, concrete strategies to help children move from what they have achieved to what we want them to achieve, teachers instead simply reiterate the desired goal – a reminder prompt. For example, *'You need to improve these two long sentences'* merely reiterates the learning goal of *'To be able to write effective long sentences'*. Better advice would be, for instance, *'Improve these two long sentences, using some short noun phrases, such as "old features", "thin blue lips", "grating voice" or similar.'* Giving 'for instances' and specific advice is key to the quality of an improvement suggestion.

(d) Children make the improvement in lesson time

The traditional model of feedback is to make suggestions for improvement which one hopes will be taken account of when the same learning objective is revisited at a later date. The main reason that comments appear over and over again on children' work is because children have not had an opportunity either to (*a*) carry out the improvement on that piece of work, according to the specificities of the improvement suggestion, whether oral or written, or (*b*) revisit the skill in another context quickly enough. Only when this takes place will the improvement become embedded and able to be applied in further contexts. As Black and Wiliam (1998) found: *'For assessment to be formative, the feedback information has to be **used**.'*

(e) Relinquishing control

In most classrooms, the *teacher* defines the goal, judges the achievement and tries to close the gap between achieved and desired performance. We need to model effective feedback, what it means to identify an improvement need, and then make a suitable improvement, aiming to gradually relinquish control so that children are trained to be effective self- and peer markers and assessors.

3. Strategies for enabling self- and peer evaluation and effective feedback *during lessons*

> *One of the reasons peer assessment is so valuable is because children often give and receive criticisms of their work more freely than in the traditional teacher/child interchange. Another advantage is that the language used by children to each other is the language they would naturally use, rather than "school" language.*

(Black et al, 2003)

Our aim is, of course, to involve children as far as possible in the analysis and constructive criticism of their own work. If the teacher is the only person giving feedback, the balance is wrong and the children become powerless, with no stake in their learning. What is more, marking is, in those circumstances, time-consuming, unwieldy and 'end-on'.

We want children to use self-evaluation continually, so that reflection, pride in successes, modification and improvement become a natural part of the process of learning. Once trained to be able to identify success against the success criteria of a task, children can relatively easily identify their own and each other's successes. With all subjects, children can also – given the criteria and good models of excellence – make their own improvements, albeit with input from the teacher at some stage, using real or previous examples to show what constitutes 'OK' compared to 'excellent'.

The following practical strategies will now be described in detail, with teacher modelling as a key activity:

(a) checking against success criteria;

(b) discussing and comparing quality;

(c) using open success criteria or learning objectives to identify success and make improvements;

(d) using traffic lights.

(a) Checking against success criteria and correcting errors on closed elements

As described in Chapter 2, success criteria tend to be open or closed. Whether they are open or closed, a first stage for self- and peer evaluation is to encourage children to stop working for a couple of minutes in order to check that they have included the success criteria. Notice that at this stage we are not talking about how well the success criteria have been met, although every read through or revisiting (if it is a practical subject) might result in some immediate error correction or improvement as the child notices things they might otherwise have missed. The teacher might first show the children a completed piece of work (from last year/another class/generated by the teacher), whatever the subject (DT plan, art work, PE sequence, writing, mathematics, geography description, etc.) and ask them to check off the success criteria as a class, so they are confident about this stage of self-evaluation. This modelling will often need to take place with young children or with children at the beginning of this process.

If the success criteria are discrete, some teachers like to colour-code them on the whiteboard and ask children to circle the success criteria in their work as each is fulfilled. Children can, of course, tick off the elements as they check their inclusion or use any other clear checking method. If the success criteria overlap, however, checking each one off in turn may not lend itself to colour-coding or ticking. For example, I might have included three success criteria in one long sentence, making colour-circling a complicated matter, whereas circling or ticking off the different elements of a formal letter will be clear.

Peer evaluation is a perfect vehicle for children learning from each other where they have gone wrong with a closed skill and how to put it right. The following account of a Year 6 mathematics lesson by Laura Turner, from Somerford Community Primary School in Dorset, illustrates two key elements of formative assessment: the class involvement in the generation of success criteria and then, in the plenary, a description of how pairs helped each other, through peer evaluation, to sort out errors in their calculations.

Weaving the elements together: Teacher Account 4

Key focus: Peer evaluation and children generating success criteria

Weaving together:

- **effective questioning**
- **children generating success criteria**
- **self-evaluation**

- **talking partners**
- **peer assessment**
- **children using unit coverage to see where the learning is going next**

Learning Objective: To find the area of compound shapes

The lesson began with a statement on the board:

'To work out the area of a rectangle, you need the measurements of all four sides.' Agree or disagree.

The children went into their talking partners and very quickly established that they did not need all four measurements because '*Two of them [the sides] are the same, you can just times them*'. During the discussion that followed, the misconceptions and confusions between area and perimeter became very apparent. The children were clearly confused about the difference. Therefore before we went any further, we needed to establish success criteria for area. In order to produce success criteria, you have to work through a problem and jot down the criteria as you go along. It really helps later when you might have forgotten what to do, because you can picture yourself working on the success criteria and it helps you remember where to start.

The children decided to begin with a rectangle. The measurements were very simple, '*because we need to keep things simple*' said one child! The children in their talking partners had two minutes to come up with anything and everything they knew that would help them understand area. I got: *surface area, amount of surface area enclosed within a 2D shape, measured in square units, formula for area is length x breadth, squared cm is cm x cm like*

(continued)

5 squared is 5 x 5! The class is very comfortable with using and drawing up success criteria, so during their discussion they were beginning to put the criteria together themselves and construct some form of list. Previous learning was becoming activated through this process. A lot of *'Oh yeah, I remember this now'* was heard! We worked through as a group to find the area of a simple rectangle, whilst putting the criteria in child speak.

This is what we came up with:

Remember to:

- *measure the length and the breadth accurately – or use the measurements given to you;*
- *check the measurements are enough – ask: Do I need to work out a missing measurement?*
- *multiply the length by the breadth;*
- *include the squared measurement in the answer;*
- *check you have answered the problem.*

In other lessons, I may ask a group to devise their own success criteria – for example with addition and subtraction, concepts most children are happy with by Year 6. However, during this lesson, by actually breaking the problem down into step-by-step instructions or ingredients, the children were being forced to be specific and precise in their understanding. I have found that it is a really good tool to establish who knows why and what they actually need to do and when. It can also highlight a lack of understanding in the use of vocabulary. This particular class were passive learners when I first had them in September, but they are now extremely good at assessing their own learning and take great pleasure in improving and using the strategies we have learned. They are also very critical learners now, and want their work to be of a certain standard and understanding – half-measures are not good enough anymore!

Having established the success criteria, we moved on to the next concept: to calculate the area of a shape formed from two rectangles, a compound shape. I put two rectangles on the board of different sizes (not attached to each other, yet!) and asked the children in their talking partners to work out both areas using the success criteria. This was done quickly. I then asked them to discuss the question *'If I put the two shapes together to form a larger shape, does the area of the shape change?'* This immediately threw a few pairs, until they saw that the rectangles were exactly the same area just put together! One child informed us we needed to include this in the success criteria, so we moved back and included:

- *Partition the shape into separate rectangles if necessary.*
- *Add the partitioned areas together.*

Happy with this, the children were then able to move on to book work and come up with some of their own examples of putting rectangles together and partitioning them in order to find the area.

(continued)

The plenary consisted of peer improvements. This class used to dislike this method and it took a lot of encouragement and role play for them to see how much more useful it is to have their work marked by a peer than me!

The children were given an example on the board and asked to work on their own for a few minutes and work out the area. They exchanged their work with their talking partner, who then marked this using the success criteria. It was interesting to see that the children did not go straight to the answer. They looked first at the success criteria and ticked off whether their partner had used it and how effectively. Having done that, they then looked at the answer to see if they had got it right. In some cases, the answer was wrong. Josh (low achiever) discovered his partner (middle/high achiever) had got the answer wrong, so he worked through the success criteria until he was able to highlight the mistake: *'Ryan partitioned the shape but then used the wrong measurement for one of the shapes.'* He then circled in Ryan's book the mistake and gave him an improvement: *'Remember to use the right measurement for the partitioned shape when finding out the area (of a compound shape).'* I wrote this in the maths book for Josh, but he told me *what* to write!

Having marked each other's books, the talking partners shared their findings with each other and discussed their improvements together. Finally, I asked them to use the self-evaluation cards to discuss their learning.

The comments I got were:

'I found the partitioning easy but then I got lost because I could not work out how to find the missing measurement.'
'The success criteria helped but I wanted more in there about finding the missing measurement. It didn't help us do that.'
'I couldn't do this at the beginning, but now I can use the success criteria and my talking partner and I can do it!'
'Area is really easy, I liked working on someone's work and finding an improvement then helping them see how they could improve.'

When I asked the children what they would remember about the maths lesson, the general consensus was:

- The success criteria – *'It gives me a formula to work from.'*
- The improvements their TP gave were really useful and helped them to see where the problem went wrong or right.
- The process they went through to get to a clear understanding of finding the area of compound shapes!

The children were aware of their learning and also where they had to improve, not just in their own learning but in their assessment of themselves and their talking partner. One child said *'I think all this helps because we can see where we need to go next and how we can achieve it. We can move forward in our learning.'*

(continued)

The children have really been set alight by formative assessment, although it has taken a long time to get there. Now they feel liberated and in control of their own learning. They are able to see how they learn, and in which direction they need to move to achieve more. At the end of the lesson, the children looked at their mind map (an overview of the term's Numeracy planning) and were delighted to see what the next step was: another lesson on area but looking at how the formula $l \times b$ can be used to find the area of a triangle. Already they were moving themselves forward and were excited by it . . . not something I believed would happen when I first began working with this group of children.

With thanks to Laura Turner, Somerford Community Primary School (Dorset Learning Team)

(b) Discussing and comparing quality

One of the most powerful ways of modelling what you want children to do is to use real examples of completed work, either on an OHP or by using an interactive whiteboard. With the whole class, success criteria can be generated, ticked off and discussed or presented to the children, then the piece analysed to see if the criteria have been met and how well they have been met.

With two contrasting finished pieces (say, an excellent piece and an average piece), however, we can go much further, and engage the children in thinking about which piece represents the most effective achievement, and why. It is important to be very specific in this process – to isolate individual success criteria, words or phrases, so that quality can be rigorously discussed, rather than asking general questions of the class, such as *'Which piece/paragraph is most effective?'*

Two Year 6 pieces from the same class and the same lesson are used now to model the process a teacher might go through to engage children in a discussion about quality (Figs 5.1 and 5.2). I have deliberately chosen pieces which, at first reading, are not what they seem. Analysing against learning objectives and success criteria forces you to focus on the *purpose* of the piece, rather than its superficial features, which is a more immediate instinct.

Fig. 5.1

> *Dear Mother,*
>
> *Life in the country is strange and mysterious. When father left I wept with tears that never seemed to disappear. The station was noisy and full of children and inside me I was screaming for you. Oh mother how I needed you. When you read this letter I hope you will understand why. When I boarded the train it was as though I was entering Hell. I sat next to a girl who was far to excited to care. She just babbled on about her granma who lived in the country and I felt sick, painfully lonely and tired. The train journey seemed to last for weeks though it was only a few hours. When I breathed the fresh air outside the train, I felt relieved.*
>
> *We, (me and the children) were taken to a large hall and waited for the villagers to come and choose a child to foster. A number of children also came in with the adults. Hour after hour and still no one looked at me. After a while I understood why. A lot of girls were wearing large ponytails and ribbons and party frocks. With my black dress and cotton cardigan I didn't stand a chance. It made me sick to think people were judging me by my clothes.*
>
> *By evening I was the only child left. Suddenly two ladies came in and took me. Miss Honeychurch and Miss Silver. They were very young, but very kind. I sleep in the attic which is very compatable. I cried when I wrote this letter. Missing you more than anything.*
>
> *Yours Karen*

Fig. 5.2

Dear Mum

I am really missing you and dad.

How is everyone back home? have you heard anything from dad yet. Mum have you joned your new job at the factory yet? On the train I was sceard and my stumch was terning, and I felt sick and lonely.

When we got to parker stasion I had to wait for my techer to go and get Mr and Mrs Brown to come and get me. I was rally wroied what they would be like but when they came and got me they seemed really nice and kind. I can not wait till the war is over and then I can come home and see you all. My room is butiful and my bed is comtobul, but my bed back home is even more comtubal their is a mirror a pear of chestterdraws and a wardrobe.

I am starting a new school next week but I am really wroied that the children won't like me at all I am not good at making new friends Send my love to dad when you hear from him and Nan and Grandad Eve.

I am staying at a farm with Mr and Mrs Brown their are cows, sheeps, chickens and duck and lots more anyway I must go now see you when the war is over

Love Lyentte xxxx

P.S. Pleas write back I'll look fawrod from hearing from you bye.

The learning objective for each piece is:

To express empathy for a character in writing.

The context is a letter home from an evacuee detailing the very beginning of the experience. The success criteria:

Include at least two of these:

■ use a range of senses;

■ use powerful adjectives and verbs to express emotion;

■ include key aspects of the experience that might make the character anxious/relieved, etc;

■ try to convey empathy between mother and daughter/son.

There are many ways we could compare the two pieces. We could, for instance, just focus on the second success criterion – *use powerful adjectives and verbs to express emotion* – and the first piece would quite definitely win out in terms of quality. Or we could stand back and assess the piece against the learning objective only: *to express empathy for a character.* Where do we think the pieces do this the best? Where do we find ourselves with a lump in the throat as we read?

Taking the first piece (Fig 5.1), we can see wonderful description, good handwriting and sophisticated phrasing. The author takes care to make her mother suffer with her – no emotions are spared: *'I wept with tears that never seemed to disappear, inside me I was screaming for you, oh mother, how I needed you . . ..'* The writing is good – there appears to be real empathy for the plight of the evacuee.

Look at the second piece (Fig 5.2) and, at first read through, it seems simple by comparison, immature and lacking description and emotion. But look carefully . . .

Points made by teachers on my one-day courses, having carefully analysed the second piece against the learning objective:

1. It is more feasibly written by a child – with child-like phrasing and language.

2. The child has deep feelings of fear and concern about her father, which she tries to keep from the mother: *'Have you heard anything from Dad yet?'* and later on, *'Send my love to Dad when you hear from him'.* She is optimistic in her phrasing, even

though she knows he could be dead. This would be a real and dominating aspect of this child's life at this time, yet the first child makes no mention of the father.

3. She tells her mother that her bed is comfortable (as does the child in the previous piece), but she makes sure she reassures her mother that *'my bed back home is even more comfortable.'*

4. Her concern about starting a new school and not being good at making new friends are again very realistic. We can imagine feeling like this ourselves.

5. She faces the reality of the situation – she is brave: *She will see her mum when the war is over.*

6. Her P.S. expresses again her empathy with her mother and perhaps her own attempts to cheer herself up. However, the true meaning is clear: *'Please write back'* is a plea from the heart. *'I'll look forward from hearing from you'* is optimistic again, but full of understated longing.

Of course we want children to eventually include all aspects of good writing in any one piece, but, while we are developing individual skills, such as expressing empathy, it is very worthwhile to narrow the focus in this way and not be constantly praising wonderful description.

The two pieces can also be used individually for modelling success and improvement, as detailed in section *(c)* below. If we took the first piece, we might decide that any of these could possibly be deemed best successes (for that child) for empathy:

> *I wept with tears that never seemed to disappear.*
> *Inside me I was screaming for you.*
> *I felt sick, painfully lonely and tired.*
> *It made me sick to think that people were judging me by my clothes.*

A possible place to improve might be at the entrance of the two ladies. We could suggest:

> *'How did the ladies show their kindness to you? Did they carry your suitcase? Did they have a gift for you? What did they do and say?'*

or maybe:

> *'How could you change the ending of the letter to reassure your mother that you are OK and that things aren't as bad as all that?'*

After this modelling, children can be asked to write their own empathy letters. They are now well equipped to tackle the task, having seen real examples and discussed what quality means. They are also enabled to carry out peer- or self-identification of successes and possible places to improve. By including this kind of modelling at the beginning of lessons, then throughout lessons stopping and sharing successes and improvements, children are being constantly engaged in the process of active learning, review and a striving for excellence.

Angela Craig, from Fair Furlong Primary School in Bristol, writes an account of two Year 5 geography lessons with a one-hour feedback session, in which a number of key skills are explored and developed, and children and teacher used a full range of formative assessment strategies.

Weaving the elements together: Teacher Account 5

Key focus: All aspects of formative assessment

Weaving together:

- **effective questioning**
- **no hands up**
- **teacher modelling quality and providing feedback during the lesson**
- **talking partners**
- **children generating success criteria**
- **self-evaluation and improvement against success criteria**

Part 1

Learning intention	Context	Success criteria
To understand the physical and human features of a mountain environment.	Desktop publication: 'The English Lake District'.	1. Use various sources to locate information. 2. Identify physical features. 3. Identify human features. 4. Organise information effectively.

Pupils were first asked *'What things might you use to find out about a particular mountain environment?'* They were given two minutes to list their ideas with a learning partner. This was an effective way to start the lesson as all the children were immediately involved, and they are very experienced at focusing on their learning with a partner. Using the 'no hands' strategy pairs were asked to feed back an idea: these were then listed and displayed at the front of the

(continued)

classroom. I have found this to be a particularly successful strategy, though it only works well in certain circumstances. The children know that they may well be asked to contribute, but feel more confident as they are in a pair and have had time to think about their ideas.

We then discussed what the phrase *physical features* means in relation to geography. I asked them to think about this in relation to a mountain environment, and gave them three minutes to work with their learning partner and list ideas. Using the 'no hands' strategy, ideas were fed back and listed. This was repeated with the phrase *human features*. Beginning the lesson by handing the learning over to the children and ensuring that they were all immediately involved, meant that all children were on task and engaged in their own learning. I was able to support pairs and address any misconceptions immediately.

Part 2 – (this could be a separate lesson)

Only at this point did I then share the learning intentions, context and success criteria (1–3, not 4 at this stage). As you can see, we were able to use the three lists generated by the children to support us with our success criteria.

To understand the physical and human features of a mountain environment.

Context: Desktop publication: 'The English Lake District'.

Success Criteria:

1. **Use various sources to locate information**
   - Maps
   - Internet
   - Photographs
   - Text books
   - Postcards
   - Globe
   - CD-Roms

2. **Identify physical features**
   - Weather
   - Climate
   - Landscape

3. **Identify human features**
   - Tourism
   - Housing
   - Work

At this point I showed the children a model chart to collect information. Some pairs decided they would use this, whilst others devised their own. They were then given a maximum of

(continued)

forty minutes to research physical and human features of 'The English Lake District'. During this time I was able to use the success criteria to comment and feed back on the quality of work from each pair, and to use the children to model quality to one another. This is an extremely effective way of giving immediate feedback and to ensure that the children know what is expected. I use this strategy a lot in my teaching and I find it exciting to watch the children improve on their own learning there and then in a lesson. It is also brilliant to address any misconceptions.

After sharing some of our findings, we looked back at the learning intention and success criteria. We used a checklist to make sure we had everything in our success criteria.

I then introduced the fourth success criteria. I told the children that they were now going to present their information and demonstrate their understanding of the learning intention using ICT. I had already prepared a checklist to support the fourth success criteria, but there was room for the children to add to this. It was presented in a grid where they could tick as they worked.

4. **Organise information effectively**

   - ICT/Desktop publishing skills, Publisher, Word or PowerPoint.
   - Sections.
   - Accurate information.
   - Pictures.
   - Text.

Organise information effectively	
ICT/Desktop publishing skills, Publisher, Word or PowerPoint	
Sections	
Accurate information	
Pictures	
Text	

I began by showing a PowerPoint presentation that I had already prepared. Working in pairs, the children then went ahead and began work on their presentation. Again I commented on work, relating it to success criteria. I also used the data projector to model children's work as I spotted something of particular interest, again related to learning intention and success criteria. This doesn't mean that the children copy – instead it inspires them to think creatively and enhance their own learning potential.

(continued)

Part 3 – Next lesson

When they were finished, the children were asked to use their checklists to ensure they had met all of the success criteria. When this was done, each presentation was shown on the data projector. Each pair was given a checklist and they were asked to see if the presentation and that particular pair had met the success criteria. The children love this, especially after a break (maybe the next day). They have learned how to comment supportively on their own and others' learning. My marking was then complete as we had all been involved in marking each others' work and the children felt that they had immediate feedback and recognition of focused learning. Time was then given to make any adjustments in the light of feedback. I felt very happy that my pupils had completed a high quality piece of work that had been marked and was focused on learning.

With thanks to Angela Craig, Fair Furlong Primary School (Bristol Learning Team)

(c) Using open success criteria or learning objectives to identify success and make improvements

Training children to identify their successes and make improvements cannot be a 'quick fix'. Part of a lesson, or follow-up to a lesson, needs to consist of modelling, from an anonymous piece of completed work, or from one of the children's own attempts, how to identify success (best places) and improvement. An example of a detailed run-through of this process now follows (Table 5.1). The subject is Literacy and the children are in Year 2. The learning objective:

To create an effective fairytale opening

Notice that there are two main elements to this learning objective: the opening and the fairytale genre, so the success criteria will need to include both. Typical success criteria might be:

Remember to include:

- The setting – where and when
- A character
- Good description
- Typical fairytale ingredients

Table 5.1

On the OHP/interactive whiteboard:	Teacher might say:
One day there was a carsle with a beautiful princess lived in there. The carsle had silver emerleds round it and the ground had gold sand around it. It looked louvly.	*'Look at the success criteria and spend one minute with your talking partner to decide whether all the success criteria can be ticked off for this child's work.'* Class establishes that all have been met: *'One day'* for the time *'A castle'* for the fairytale place *'A princess'* for the fairytale character *'Beautiful'* and the description of the castle are effective
One day there was a carsle with a beautiful princess lived in there. The carsle had silver emerleds round it and the ground had gold sand around it. It looked louvly.	*'Now which do we think are the three very best places in this writing? We will circle the three best bits, but first one minute with your talking partner.'*
One day there was a carsle with a beautiful princess lived in there. (The carsle had) (silver emerleds round it) and the ground had gold sand around it. It looked louvly.	*'No hands up – I'm going to ask a few different pairs . . .* **'The castle had silver emeralds round it.'** *'Who agrees that that is a good bit?Why?'* *'Yes, it is very good description – let's circle it.'* *'Now for a second-best bit . . .'*
One day there was a carsle with (a beautiful princess) lived in there. (The carsle had) (silver emerleds round it) and the ground had gold sand around it. It looked louvly.	**'Beautiful princess.'** *'How many pairs agree with that? We know a little bit about her and princesses in fairy tales are usually beautiful aren't they? OK – let's circle that bit too.'* *'Let's agree a third place. It could be any of the things left. We have more description or we could choose the place or the time. What do you think?'*
One day (there was a carsle)	*'OK. Let's circle "***there was a castle***".'*

(continued)

On the OHP/interactive whiteboard:	Teacher might say:
with a beautiful princess lived in there. The carsle had silver emerleds round it and the ground had gold sand around it. It looked louvly. One day there was a carsle with a beautiful princess lived in there. * The carsle had silver emerleds round it and the ground had gold sand around it. It looked louvly.	*'Now. Where do we think this piece could be improved? What do we have most information about? Yes, the castle. So what could we help this child improve? One minute with talking partners . . ..'* *'So we have two ideas – more about the princess or more about the time. Let's do more about the princess . . .'.* *'Now, here are two ways we could help the child . . . we could give them some ideas or we could actually write another sentence or two for them.' For instance, we could say to the child:* **'What is her name? What makes her beautiful? How old is she?'** **(A scaffolded prompt – giving ideas and suggestions)** *or we could suggest she writes something like:* **'The princess was eight years old with long red hair, green eyes and a smile which made young princes faint.' (An example prompt – you write it for them as a possible option.)** *'Two minutes with your talking partner to decide what you think would be good to help the child improve this bit–we want her to add some more after the sentence about the princess, where I've put the asterix.'*
One day there was a carsle with a beautiful princess lived in there. * The carsle had silver emerleds round it and the ground had gold sand around it. It looked louvly. *Her name was Annabelle.* *She had long blonde hair and deep blue eyes but her nose was always stuck in the air.*	*'So, we've talked about our ideas and helped this child write a bit more about the princess. After we've talked with her about it, she then writes the improvement herself at the end of the piece, otherwise she'd find it hard to fit it in, wouldn't she? Now, you've all all done this before, so you know the first thing to do is to decide where you think your three best bits are . . ..'*

Children are now asked to identify their own three best successes and either circle them or underline them in pink or some other device. Pinks (for successes) and underlining in green (for an improvement) are popular methods (pink for tickled pink and green for growth!) because pink and green pencils can be permanently available on children's tables.

The success and improvement strategy has a suggested starting point of two or three successes and one improvement per child. This orthodoxy is a necessary training stage. Eventually, of course, we want children to be able to identify any number of successes or improvement needs in their work, but, in the initial stages, for most day-to-day work, focusing on only a few elements allows greater development of the skill or concept in question.

Children might then be asked to work in pairs discussing their successes and agreeing them or changing their minds.

For children used to this process, they can now move on to identifying a place to improve and talking together about how to make that improvement. There are many options: children can sometimes make the improvement completely on their own; they can simply talk to each to each other about the possible improvements, then write them on their own; or they can swap work and write an improvement suggestion to each other, swap back and make the improvement. The middle of the lesson can usefully be used to read out some children's improvements. While children are engaged in identifying successes or improvements, the teacher can be talking with individuals or pairs, adding her own thoughts and ideas and looking for good examples to read out during or at the end of the lesson. Reading out interesting examples during the course of the lesson is more useful to children who are still thinking about their improvements.

Emma Goff, from St James' C of E Infant School in Tunbridge Wells, next takes us through an excellent description of two consecutive Year 2 lessons in which, first of all, a stimulating drama context inspires children's writing – a vital first stage. She then uses some paired writing from the class to model success and improvement, focusing on one success criterion. Through talking partners, the children go through the process of identifying their own success and making improvements. Notice the importance of the focus on only one success criterion. By narrowing the focus in this way, the children's understanding and development throughout the lesson is maximised.

Weaving the elements together: Teacher Account 6

Key focus: Peer evaluation/marking using success and improvement

Weaving together:

- **teacher modelling success and improvement using a real example**
- **peer assessment/marking**

- **talking partners**
- **children making own improvements during the lesson**

YEAR 2 (30 children)

Lesson One: Using drama to contextualise the writing

Context

Literacy; Drama and Writing in role (Two consecutive lessons)

In order to provide a purposeful context for writing and a real audience for response, I engaged my class through extended process drama. This involves 'living inside' a text, taking on a variety of different roles to develop a more informed understanding of the characters and events in the story. Through this context the children are able to experience the situations, and begin to make connections with issues in their own lives.

Learning Intentions:

To write in role as a book character:
- to recognise feelings and emotions
- to understand choices characters make and their reasons
- to appreciate relationships between characters

Success Criteria

My writing includes feelings, emotions and reasons that explain a character's actions.

Using the text *Rose meets Mr Wintergarten*, by Bob Graham, my class and I became immersed in a fictional reality. The story begins with the Summers family moving into a new home which happens to be next door to a rather dark and forbidding mansion house, surrounded by menacing barbed wire fencing. The children took on roles of the family, including the young daughter, Rose. They physically began organising their new home, hanging pictures, organising furniture and planting up the garden. They gossiped in role as children who lived in the neighbourhood, telling tales about Mr Wintergarten (whom no one

(continued)

had ever seen with their own eyes!). However, it is during a game of football, when the ball flies high up over the fencing and into the realms of the unknown, where the story really begins to unfold. The children took on the role of Rose, accompanied by her Mum, who enters the grounds of her unknown neighbour bearing flowers and home-made cakes. She is immediately confronted by a dog (who she pacifies with the cakes) before continuing to the front door. With the teacher in role as Mr Wintergarten, the children tentatively enter the house on his command and ask for their ball back. The curtains are closed, it's cold. He glares down at Rose from his dinner table and demands she *'Clear off!'*

I narrated the next part of the story, ad-libbing Rose running from the house in tears and Mr Wintergarten uncharacteristically venturing outside onto his front doorstep to scribble a note to Rose. In role as Mr Wintergarten, the children shared thoughts about the situation and explanations for their actions through a variety of drama conventions – e.g. thought tracking (speaking thoughts out loud) and decision alley (listening to a range of alternatives to help make a choice). They invented reasons to explain their unkempt appearance, vicious pet dog, dirty house and overgrown garden. At this point we began writing in role. Some children chose to work independently, others worked together in twos. We later continued within the frame of the same dramatic context so that the children could receive the letter in role as Rose. I felt that this would provide the opportunity to provoke a genuine, affective response. To maintain the momentum of the previous lesson I decided to do this in the next session, later the same morning.

Lesson Two: Marking for improvement

Oral feedback often seems most appropriate when working with infants, although the number of children requiring this focused support at the same time can make it a challenging task! For this reason I regularly involve the children in the process of evaluating their work collaboratively with a response partner. My role in supporting the children is to provide a very clear model for identifying successes and improvements.

Learning Intention:

To make improvements to writing
• to add detail
• to explain reasoning
• to make the purpose clear
• to provoke a response from the intended audience

Success Criteria (as lesson one):

My writing includes feelings, emotions and reasons that explain the character's actions.

Using the following example of Rosie and Natalie's writing, copied onto OHP acetate, I began by modelling the process of improving writing with the whole class,

(continued)

To Rose,
I am sorry I scared you. *I will send you back your ball*. I will be friends with you. My house is so dark because the sun light can't get to it. *My dog is not bad even if he is big*. Can you come every day? **I've had no children for ten years**. *Do you forgive me?*
Love Mr Wintergarten

The children discussed their immediate responses to the letter with their talking partners. I felt it significant that at this point the children's talk was completely focused on the content of the letter, as opposed to secretarial issues. Working together again as a whole class, we identified a section – a phrase or sentence – of the letter which made us (in role as Rose) 'tickled pink'. The children's suggestions are marked with italics. We finally agreed that the concluding question *'Do you forgive me?'* was particularly important, as it demanded a response from Rose. The children's insights included *'He's changed his mind. I think he is sorry'* and *'It will make Rose feel happy'*. This was significant for me because the children had changed their initial subjective opinions about Mr Wintergarten.

Again working initially with their partners, the children suggested ideas where the letter needed 'green for growth'. The class overwhelmingly chose *'I've had no children for ten years'*. Reasons included *'He needs to explain more why he hasn't had any children for so long'* and *'He needs to make it clearer that he was going to give the ball back.'* I was amazed by Harry's initial suggestion for improvement, which reads *'My wife took my children away. No one has wanted me for a long time. It makes me so sad and nearly breaks my heart!'* As I wrote his narrated words onto the OHP there was an unusual silence and even a gasp from one of the children! His powerful explanation could suggest how, through immersion in role, he was able to appreciate the context that frames this realistic experience.

With these examples in mind, the children began re-reading their work with their response partners, both in the assumed role of Rose. They circled one successful section in pink and one section for development in green. The following letters show the successes (*Tickled pink shown in italic print*) and improvements (**Green for growth shown in bold**) that the children enthusiastically identified (independently of adult support). They wrote the improvements straight away, which only took about five minutes.

Interestingly, Rosie and Natalie's writing showed different success and improvement to the ones suggested by the class. They were tickled pink with the sentence *'I will send your ball back'* and decided to improve *'Can you come every day?'* with *'Can you come once a week to comfort me? I promise I will not scare you.'*

Michael and Mobin:

Dear Rose,
I'm sorry for yelling at you. Shall I tell you why I was so grumpy? I never had anyone to live with or any children. I was so lonely all my life! **Now I am not lonely because you are living next door and you're very kind**.
From Mr Wintergarten

(continued)

Improvement: I'm still a bit grumpy because you've only been once. I haven't had visitors in years. Can you visit me more often?

Mary and Amy:

Dear Rose,
I'm so sorry that I wouldn't give your ball back. Sorry that I said so many terrible words. I know why they call me names because everybody thinks I am mean, horrible and terrifying. **My plants are so overgrown because I never go outside which means I never get to cut them.**
Best wishes from Mr Wintergarten.

Improvement: My plants are so overgrown because I never go outside because I am scared the kids will tease me. So I don't get to cut them.

Fran:

Dear Rose

I am very sorry I shouted. **It's just people make fun of me because I am blue and they make fun of my long nose. I am blue because I'm cold.** If you want you can have your ball back. *If you like you can come to tea.* I will clean my house, paint, dust, vacuum and tidy!
From Mr Wintergarten

Improvement: I am blue because I stay up all night being sad, worried and lonely. I wonder why people make fun of my nose? I am also blue because I am so cold.

Considering these pieces of writing, I felt that the children had successfully written in role. However, I was particularly pleased with the way the children's improvements met the success criteria of *'My writing includes feelings, emotions and reasons that explain the character's actions.'* My intention had been to enable the children to add detail to writing, to explain reasoning, to make the purpose clear and to provoke a response from the intended audience. The children's improvements could suggest a deeper understanding of the character's intentions and context. They successfully appreciate feelings and emotions, and make thoughtful, reasoned choices that show an appreciation of the relationships between characters.

With thanks to Emma Goff, St James' C of E Infant School (Tonbridge Learning Team)

(d) Use of traffic lights

For creating a formative dialogue

For some time, teachers have experimented with 'traffic lights' as a way of getting children to rate their achievement (green for achieved, amber for half-achieved, red for not achieved: need help). Where traffic lights are used summatively in this way, I believe they have little useful impact. It is when they are used to enable a formative dialogue about achievement that the mechanism becomes useful.

Problems about leaving traffic lights till the end of the lesson are:

■ Children who are over-confident tend to over-estimate their achievement. Similarly, less confident children tend to under-estimate their achievement.

■ The comparison effect is explicitly set up. At a glance, children can see how they appear to be doing compared to others.

■ If a child puts a red at the end of their work, this must be the fault of the teacher, not the child. Either the work was inappropriately modelled or was completely mismatched to the child's ability. The time to seek help is during the process of the lesson or while the work is being done. The end is too late! There may, of course, be exceptional circumstances where a child believed they knew what they were doing for homework, but at the time found it difficult.

■ With open-skill success criteria (where there is no definite answer, but a continuum of quality) there are further problems. If I feel I have succeeded at three out of five success criteria really well, is that amber? What if I had achieved all five criteria but without much quality? How about if I met only two criteria but, in the case of English writing, wrote a more powerful piece than if I had attended to them all?

A5 traffic light cards on children's tables encourage them to be used during lessons as a means of making some kind of judgement about achievement *so far*. Either with a talking partner or with an adult, children might be asked to focus on one of the success criteria and point to which colour best represents their achievement or feeling about how they are doing at this moment for that particular element or stage of the work. This encourages children to express any difficulties while the lesson is in progress, and seek help without fear of failure or embarrassment.

For rating existing knowledge

At the beginning of a unit of work which is very knowledge-based, such as history, geography or science, it can be useful to ask children to traffic light a given list of key facts they will be learning according to:

Red – I don't know this yet.

Amber – I know something about this.

Green – I know this already.

As the topic progresses, the traffic lighting can be repeated.

As a way in to group evaluation

Another useful strategy at Key Stage 2 is to ask children, at the end of a unit of work, to talk to the people in their group for, say, two minutes about one aspect of a unit of work which they have found particularly interesting. Each person in the group scores the child's oral account in private, using a traffic-light system to compare the talk with how they feel they, themselves, could have explained the same thing:

Green – *meaning* Better than I could have explained it.

Amber – *meaning* About as well as I could have explained it.

Red – *meaning* Not as well as I could have explained this.

When all the talks in the group are completed, each child in turn then has their 'scores' revealed. At this stage, if any child has awarded a red or green to somebody, they have to explain to the speaker what they thought was particularly poor or particularly good about the talk.

It is here that teachers have found that children are not only very honest, but are able to discover their own strengths and weaknesses – and not just from the talker. It may be other children who raise items that have been forgotten.

4. The role of teacher marking

I have written a great deal about teacher marking in my previous books, especially in *Enriching Feedback in the Primary Classroom* (2003), which focuses mainly on this aspect of formative assessment. However, formative assessment constantly updates itself as teacher's feedback and experimentation reveal more about what really helps children's learning. That is not to say that examples of teacher marking have not been useful, but we are now entering an era where incorporating these things into lessons is the clear way forward.

The dilemma has been constant: how to match high quality marking with manageability. The answer has developed logically over the last few years. There is a limit to how much time a teacher can spend on quality (e.g. 'success and improvement') marking away from the children. In terms of children's learning and progress, it is clear that marking away from children and then finding time for them to make improvements has far less impact than incorporating success and improvement into actual lessons, with teacher modelling as a vital component. Of course, quality marking away from children has, nevertheless, proved to be spectacularly successful in many schools, with noticeable progress made in children's writing. However, it has always been at the expense of teacher's time, unless it is integrated into lessons.

This chapter has developed the integrated approach in detail, and, feedback from the Learning Teams confirms that this must be the way forward. We need to format lessons so that children are constantly reviewing their work. They need clear models of how to identify success against specific criteria, suggestions for how to improve and opportunities for discussions about quality through comparing pieces of contrasting worth, regardless of the subject.

Teacher marking can then become a final look at improvements carried out in lessons, maybe adding comments at that stage, knowing that the real work, thinking and value have already happened.

When work can be profitably **marked together** in a whole-class setting (e.g. closed exercises such as mathematics or sentence-level work) this cuts out a layer of often unnecessary marking, where wrong answers simply demoralise children and are, once again, too late to be pointed out. By giving children fewer items to do in the first place, then stopping to go through the answers and related processes, children can mark their own work, self-correcting where necessary, thus enhancing the learning possibilities. Again, teacher marking then becomes a final check.

On a regular basis, teachers usually find it useful to **create a 'test' or application opportunity** for children to bring all their learning together, such as a whole story, maths investigation, science experiment, art where there is a choice from a number of learnt techniques and so on. This marking is usually better if focused around some kind of summary feedback for children about where their strengths and weaknesses lie, rather than a detailed overmark of all the criteria ever learnt.

Any rethink about marking needs to be reflected in school policies, with accompanying rationale based on experimentation and teacher's findings. We are gradually becoming clearer about what activities it is worth teachers investing time in, and what traditions need to be rethought and reworked.

Learning Team findings about 'success and improvement' within lessons

Overall, teachers said that the impact of this approach had been that children were realising their needs through higher-order thinking, focusing more noticeably on success criteria and automatically self-evaluating.

Reception/Year 1

- Introducing success and improvement led naturally to self-evaluation.

- Some teachers began by getting children into talking partners and asking them to tell each other how to improve. This led to children seeing that all children have a need to improve, and they were keen to help each other. They liked pinks and greens.

- Very empowering for lower achievers because seeing success in one area motivated them to achieve in another.

- It was very effective to give oral feedback part way through a lesson (using whole class and talking partners) – it was the first time one teacher saw the children get off their seats and look properly at the success criteria.

- Year 1 – big impact using pinks and greens and very useful to compare two pieces of work.

- The children saw that it is better to be proud of your work after you've made an improvement.

- Children are more involved, talking more about their work, more keen to make it better.

Year 2

- It has to be planned into the middle of a lesson.
- It is important to know what makes a good piece of work, so discussing quality is vital.
- It is becoming second nature for children to self-evaluate.
- It is important to use anonymous pieces first, although it helps to give them names.
- The biggest impact came from giving children time to make improvements, rather than the teacher doing loads of marking.
- Very motivating for children.
- It is important for the teacher to make a decision to work with one piece in depth than to try to cover everything.
- Children's work has improved and SAT results gone up. Some made improvements to their work during the test!
- Children are proving to be more analytical than teachers previously thought.

Years 3, 4 and 5

The previous feedback *plus* . . .

- Very successful for 'Using & Applying' mathematics.
- It needs a whole-school approach for maximum impact.
- It takes children a long time to make really effective suggestions (more modelling needed).
- Children need to know what constitutes a very good piece.
- Analysing a piece of work has been more effective than the usual teacher input.
- This approach encourages children to seek help during the task.

Year 6

- Vital that this approach is integrated into lessons and children become skilled self- and peer evaluators.
- Important to tick off success criteria then discuss quality and improvement.

- There are no longer problems about what to do when 'finished'.

- This is massive cultural change – it's not just a strategy change.

Summary

- Feedback needs to be focused on the learning objective of the task and not on comparisons with other children.

- Verbal and non-verbal language from the teacher give powerful messages to the child about his or her ability.

- Grading *every* piece of work leads to demoralisation for lower achievers and complacency for higher achievers.

- We need to give *specific* feedback focusing on success and improvement, rather than correction.

- We need to focus improvement suggestions on closing the gap between current and desired performance.

- Children need opportunities to make improvements on their work.

- We need to train children to effectively self- and peer assess.

- Marking away from children has less value than incorporating in lessons modelling of quality and specific improvements, followed by self- and peer evaluation and subsequent improvements.

- It is extremely effective to model success and improvement and compare quality using contrasting examples of anonymous work.

- Aim for children constructively marking their own work against the learning objective/success criteria of the task, sometimes with a partner.

- Children need to be trained, in stages, to mark their own and each others' work.

- There need to be ground rules about paired marking to avoid anxiety.

- Success criteria should be a first-stage focus of self-assessment, and where the success criteria are open, improvements can be modelled, discussed and made in lesson time.

- Traffic lights are best used to initiate an on-the-spot, formative rather than summative dialogue about achievement.

INSET suggestions

1. After reading this chapter, involve staff in discussions about strengths and potential development areas. Share ideas about existing practice for self- and paired evaluation and marking.
2. Demonstrate modelling the success and improvement strategy in a staff meeting, as outlined on pages 101–3. Staff will be supported by reading Teacher Account 6.
3. Ask staff to trial, in this order:
   - using an anonymous piece for involving the whole class in deciding whether the success criteria have been fulfilled;
   - using that piece for whole-class identification of success and improvement against either the learning objective or one of the success criteria, making paired suggestions for improvement;
   - using two contrasting pieces to analyse, with the whole class, which success criteria are most effectively achieved and why (remember to focus in on specific small sections).
4. Trial some of the specific ideas for self- and peer evaluation outlined here and feed back findings.

6 Headteacher and LEA perspectives

Key messages for all those involved in the development of formative assessment

1. The Headteacher perspective

The significance of leadership has long been recognised as pivotal in effecting lasting and deep change in our schools. Many individual teachers become inspired to experiment with formative assessment, and can have enormous influence on other teachers in the school, but, if we want whole-school commitment to formative assessment, the role of the headteacher and senior management team is to lead and spearhead its development. There needs to be a Senior Management Team vision for the future of the ethos and culture of the school, in which honest opinions are expressed:

- *Is it to be a performance culture or a learning culture?*

- *Will teachers be allowed to take risks in experimenting with formative assessment?*

- *Do we have the courage to let teachers drop unnecessary planning or marking in order to focus on new ways of working which better facilitate children's learning and teachers' teaching?*

- *Are we prepared to take on possible complete revamping of planning or rewrites of assessment policies?*

- *Can we commit to a long period of trialling and feedback, and support teachers in this development by giving them planning and discussion time?*

I asked two headteachers from the Dorset Learning Team – Phil Minns, from Ferndown First School, and Adam Parsons, from

St Gregory's C of E Primary School – to write a summary of the ways in which they had led staff in developing formative assessment (it is rare to have headteachers attending, but these two wanted to be there to support the project by working alongside their teachers and experimenting themselves in the classroom). The accounts reveal similarities and differences – typical, of course, of the range of approaches across the country.

School development: Headteacher Account 1

Identifying the key aspect of teaching and learning that will make the fundamental difference to the progress and attainment of our pupils can feel like trying to find one needle in a very large and very full needle warehouse. Not only is it difficult, but you're never quite sure if you've got the right one.

We participated in the Assessment for Learning project led by Shirley Clarke for our LEA to help us identify why we had underachievement when we had such a hard-working team of teachers and teaching assistants. Staff were working really hard, but children were just not making the progress they deserved. As a result of this work, we have refocused our attention on what quality learning and teaching are, and are using this to re-evaluate how we work.

How does it fit in the big picture?

Here are some of the ideas that had real resonance with key issues facing our school:

■ **Untapped potential, not fixed IQ** – the idea that we all have untapped potential is personally reassuring (the outlook for my school is worrying if this is as good as I'll get!). Everyone has the potential to learn and improve: we just have to create the environment in which it can happen.
■ **The enemy of learning is coverage** – we need to move away from a *delivery* model of education toward one which focuses on *learning* and identifying next steps.
■ **Intrinsic motivation** – teaching and learning are fundamentally enjoyable and rewarding activities, yet the motivation and engagement of our pupils and staff remain central to why many of our pupils underachieve.
■ **Learned helplessness** – we know in school that some children find it very hard to work independently, and we need to question, particularly with our younger children, if we can honestly say they can do something if they can't do it on their own.

(continued)

■ **It's not about how do we fit it all in, it's about rethinking what we do** – we have to rethink much of what we do. We have created a set of beliefs about what good teachers do (plan all day Sunday, mark every piece of written work a child attempts, carry large boxes home every night . . .) that *prevent* us from actively enabling children to learn.

Where did we start?

We started by exploring with our staff the idea of removing the context from the learning intention to ensure one clear learning intention for every lesson. We have teachers who work really hard and put a lot of effort into their planning; however, we were not getting the progress we felt we should expect. When we began to look at our learning intentions we began to realise just how hard we were making it for our children to learn. The emphasis on the context – *retell the story of **Little Red Riding Hood*** – resulted in children seeing every lesson as new and different rather than the re-visiting of a previously taught skill – ***retell the story*** of Little Red Riding Hood.

At the same time, we introduced the idea of success criteria. One of the issues that we had identified from lesson observations was that activities within lessons were often lacking the learning impact of other parts of the lesson. We felt that using success criteria would strengthen the 'thread' of learning throughout the lesson, by enabling teachers to focus on what they want the children to *learn* rather than what they want the children to *do*.

How do you do it without Shirley Clarke?

We had two places on the project being run by Dorset LEA and felt that we needed to share this experience with the whole staff. We shadowed our project meetings and activities back in school with staff meetings and planned activities, but found that the greatest impact came for those of us directly involved in the action. So, for the following year, we decided to introduce professional development projects for all our teachers and teaching assistants. We planned and introduced three themed projects – Assessment for Learning, Motivation and Engagement, and Using Interactive Whiteboards – and split the staff into cross-phase 'teams'. The three school-improvement projects were intended to engage teachers and teaching assistants in shared learning and investigation, to build not only the knowledge pool within the school, but also an opportunity to learn on behalf of one another.

These projects were based on improving the quality of learning experience our children receive and used the model of action research which we enjoyed from our participation in the Shirley Clarke project. By giving staff the opportunity to reflect on their practice and access new information, they are far more likely to embed their learning in their practice.

(continued)

We chose three priorities for development which otherwise would have been a whole-school focus:

- **Assessment for Learning** - a project focusing on practice in the classroom with an emphasis on deepening the understanding of staff about how the use of Assessment for Learning practices actually impacts on the ethos and culture of the classroom.
- **Motivation and Engagement** – engaging our children in their own learning has become a thread of our school-improvement strategy. This project has concentrated on how we create the right culture for learning, seeing Assessment for Learning as more than simply a bolt-on strategy and much more as part of our learning culture.
- **Using interactive whiteboards** – This began as a purely informational project, with teachers and teaching assistants developing their own skills in using the whiteboard as a teaching tool. Inevitably, as we create a learning culture based on Assessment for Learning, this work has spilled over into areas covered by the other projects.

Overall, these projects have allowed us to explore at much greater depth three large aspects of whole-school improvement. The conversations and discussion arising from teachers and teaching assistants working together but engaged in different projects has also developed the whole-staff knowledge base as well as supporting our aim to become a learning community.

Next steps?

The feedback we had at the end of the project emphasised our own belief that we were at the *start* of something rather that at the end. It was clear that we had to make some fundamental changes to the way we were working, and that we needed to ensure the adult learning that had taken place was not lost. We introduced a new planning format that separated context from learning intention and put the planning of success criteria before any thoughts of activity. We also began to plan a new teaching and learning handbook to set down exactly how we enable learning to happen. By this stage we began to realise that we were not altering the *systems* we had in place, but were changing the *culture* of the school and our perception of what learning is.

We have begun to embed the principles of Assessment for Learning in the culture of our school because we know that it is not an add-on to good practice or even an aspect of good practice, it *is* good practice.

With thanks to Phil Minns, Ferndown First School (Dorset Learning Team)

School development: Headteacher Account 2

Background

I have been involved in a lot of work on thinking skills and developing the involvement of children in their learning. I had heard Dylan Willam at a Dorset conference and was inspired by what he was saying. I was extremely pleased to be fortunate enough to be invited by Teresa Bain to attend the action research project with Shirley. Several of my teachers were interested in the project, although only one, Rachel King, was able to attend the course with me.

Actions

We attended all four days of the action research project. We fed back at school informally on how inspiring it was and what we were trialling as a result. In the Summer term 2004 the teachers were interested in our course, so we led two staff meetings on learning intentions and success criteria. This was not part of a whole-school formulated plan but just to interest staff to reflect and have a go – assessment for learning was on the School Improvement Plan, but it was to take a greater prominence than we had planned at the time of writing.

Our whole-staff INSET for the spring term 2005 was based around feeding back on the work of Shirley and our action research findings, and to set up new action research teams across the school. Rachel and I led the input sessions using a series of PowerPoints and video clips of Rachel teaching. Although it was a watered-down version of what we had experienced, we were passionate about the benefits for the children. The teaching staff recognised this and were keen to have a go at some approaches. I suspended our usual round of scrutiny and monitoring to allow for total focus on creating the right atmosphere to have a go at some of these approaches, and purchased a copy of Shirley's *Enriching Feedback in the Primary Classroom* for each teacher.

Although my philosophy of education embraced this work wholeheartedly, and I believed that this was the way forward for the school, Rachel was the authority in this development because she was the one who had trialled it over a long period in the classroom. By the time we led the professional development sessions, some elements of the assessment for learning agenda had been a mainstay in Rachel's classroom for the best part of a year.

As a headteacher, the project excited me for two reasons. Firstly, the 'action research' approach itself offered lots of opportunities. We are at the stage of needing to empower our

(continued)

subject leaders. Offering all staff the opportunity to observe, feed back, observe good practice across key stages and act as coaches and mentors, was priceless:

'Nothing in the school has more impact on children in terms of skills development, self-confidence or classroom behaviour, than the personal and professional development of teachers.' (Barth 1990)

Secondly, the whole of the formative assessment agenda is rooted in high quality learning and teaching, our core purpose. This project affects everyone from Reception to Year 6 and some of the approaches will have a marked impact on the learning offered to the children. We structured our sessions to concentrate on:

- talking partners
- questioning
- pupil self-assessment and evaluation.

Before each session, there was a share opportunity. Each of the teachers had been put into learning partners. This would enable them to plan together, to observe each other, to feed back positively with challenge and to act as each other's mentor. In staff meetings we are not always keen to talk about the wonderful things that are happening in our own classrooms. By pairing teachers up, they were much happier to talk about the positives they had seen whilst observing their partner.

Realising that all action research projects start small, I have given each teacher an afternoon planning time, and a morning to observe their partner and prepare to give supportive but critical feedback. Aware that this is little time, I am preparing for release time for observation of good practice in the summer term. Also in the summer we will need to reflect and discuss an agreed whole-school approach and reflect this in our teaching and learning policy.

As part of a leadership programme I am doing, I have had three headteachers in to look closely at an issue in the school. I suggested to the staff that it would be very interesting to ask them to look at the impact of formative assessment on the Speaking and Listening skills of our children. The teachers were happy with this. The Assessment for Learning agenda featured on most teachers' performance management targets and oracy was a target for our literacy subject leader. Apart from the oral feedback in staff meetings, I have asked teachers as part of their performance management to do a written reflection on the impact on the learning and on their approach to teaching.

I may ask several teachers to present their action research for a full Governors' meeting. This will keep the stakeholders informed of this important initiative and allows for good professional development opportunities for the teachers.

Our Deputy is sharing the main thrust of what we are doing with the teacher assistants at their briefing meetings. One is very familiar with formative assessment from working in Rachel's classroom. Her feedback added weight to the positives of formative assessment for the children.

(continued)

Impact

The potential impact on engagement and motivation is clear. Also the effect on speaking and listening should be measurable. As it is impacting on the quality of teaching and learning, formative assessment should have a measurable increase in average points progress for all groups in each classroom.

Looking forwards

As there were two headteachers who were on the Formative Assessment project in our pyramid, we were able to persuade the rest of the headteachers to write a bid for £15000 to develop formative assessment across the pyramid. This funding comes from the DfES for networking. We await the results of this. If successful, it will allow us to embed practice through schools over the next two years and offer great opportunities for professional development.

Comments from visiting headteachers, from teachers and children:

On peer marking

'It gives me a chance to read other people's work and gives me ideas.' child
'It is better because you learn from your partner and it will help you improve your work so that when the teacher sees it she might think it is excellent.' child
'Peer pressure for the good seemed more powerful than teacher pressure to do well.' visiting head

On talking partners

'When you listen to the teacher for a long time, I can't stand it.' child
'It helps you to learn and learn to listen and get ideas.' child
'It makes learning more interesting.' child
'Good concentration and motivation and participation in the lesson.' visiting head

On questioning

'Children were very clear that questions were for thinking and discussion, with no right or wrong.' visiting head
'Everyone's a winner.' child

Of the whole-school ethos and staff

'A real learning environment, with confident children talking about learning.' visiting head
'Real evidence of staff commitment to trial this. They are motivating and challenging the children.' visiting head

With thanks to Adam Parsons, St Gregory's C of E Primary School (Dorset Learning Team)

2. The local education authority perspective

Just as the commitment and enthusiasm of the Head is central to school development of formative assessment, the LEA needs to have a similar 'champion', usually an adviser, who is passionate about formative assessment and dedicated to spreading the word. Of course, gaining appropriate funding is often key to the success of any LEA development. I have also noticed that the most successful LEAs confidently steer schools away from any unsuitable materials coming out from higher powers, and point them in the direction of resources that they believe will be helpful to schools. Other key features are:

■ finding ways of getting schools to network and share practice;

■ including as many LEA staff as possible in training so that there is a consistent message to schools;

■ setting up LEA training days;

■ involving teachers in action research with feedback sessions;

■ getting teachers to talk about and demonstrate practice to each other through LEA professional development courses or events;

■ understanding that the development of formative assessment is ongoing;

■ taking elements of formative assessment in turn and spending quality time on those aspects;

■ focusing on the keenest schools and teachers as the way in and forward.

Two LEA advisers now tell their stories: Tim Nelson from Gateshead, and Teresa Bain from Dorset.

LEA development: Account 1

The focus to develop systems of formative assessment began in late 2000 in Gateshead Primary Education. The drive to improve learning was seen as fundamental to raising standards, and the use of formative assessment was viewed as integral to this.

A whole range of initiatives were employed to develop formative assessment systems in primary education. These included:

- spreading awareness of formative assessment and how it helps to develop understanding in learning and greater pupil independence;
- involving headteachers, and key personnel in schools, and Advisory Teachers and Consultants from the 'Authority' who could help by working alongside and planning with teachers;
- raising the profile of formative assessment and encouraging the development of practice through assessment group meetings, conferences, displays, workshops and other means;
- facilitating change by reflecting upon the learning climate in schools;
- offering a model framework for the development of formative assessment, as well as documentation and action research;
- networking and sharing understanding through opportunities to discover best practice is also key to improving practice both within the local authority and with other authorities.

In December 2003, an Action Research Project was started with 16 of our schools (32 teachers) to promote the development of learning through formative assessment and related skills and techniques. This was led by Shirley, and supported and facilitated by the local authority through the inspector for assessment and consultants. This culminated with a 'showcase' in October 2004 which impressively displayed the findings and success of those involved. This has acted as an exciting catalyst for those interested in developing best practice in their own schools, both within Gateshead and beyond. Many of the teachers involved with the project have delivered sessions to others, and the project continues – investigating the use of other initiatives, meeting regularly and supported by Gateshead Consultants.

Continuing to spread awareness is a way of sharing and celebrating progress and achievements; acknowledging best practice and building upon this to the benefit of children, particularly as they move schools, is an important way of building capacity and sustainability.

(continued)

With the emergence of the Government's initiative to drive learning by using assessment for learning, the profile of day-to-day assessment and feedback in learning has heightened awareness of the usefulness of these systems.

A 'Themed Visit' took place in Gateshead in the summer term of 2004 which identified how far schools had progressed in developing the formative skills as part of learning, and where this was most effective and why.

The findings most helpful in structuring the next developments with our schools were:

- Strong leadership from the headteacher often displaying enthusiasm, knowledge and commitment to the development of effective systems of assessment and to enhance learning.
- A deputy headteacher, department head or assessment coordinator who is a very good exemplar role model, able to demonstrate excellent practice and support other staff with the implementation and development of initiatives.
- Uniformity of approach across a school or department with clear structures and a framework for the staff and children to follow.
- A collaborative whole-team involvement where teachers and support staff are enthusiastic and confident so that pupils become enthusiastic.
- A focus upon developing learning and assessment skills, where pupils' achievement is celebrated and develops self-esteem, leading to growing understanding of objectives and success criteria in their learning.
- Strong conditions and an atmosphere conducive to promoting learning.
- Productive feedback based upon the learning objective and success criteria, with useful marking systems.
- Opportunities for pupils to use these feedback comments to move their learning forward.
- Pupils respond well to day-to-day assessment, and the enthusiasm of teachers.
- The effective development if peer and self-assessment comes from raised self-esteem and improved confidence in relation to their learning.
- In special schools, indications from observations suggest that these schools are particularly strong in developing conditions for learning and in using curricular targets.

With thanks to Tim Nelson, Primary Link Inspector for Assessment, Gateshead LEA

LEA development: Account 2

Dorset LEA has had a strong history of commitment to assessment. This stretches back to the Records of Achievement Project in secondary schools during the 1980s. The LEA maintained the commitment to developing high quality assessment processes in schools by ensuring that assessment Advisers and Inspectors are part of the Pupil and School Improvement Service.

With the publication of *Inside the Black Box* by Paul Black and Dylan Wiliam in 1998, we signed up to the view expressed by Black and Wiliam that the way to develop high quality assessment practice is 'through programmes of professional development that build on existing good practice'. Many teachers did not recognise the highly effective teaching strategies which they used normally as part of everyday teaching, as assessment. The increasing emphasis on high-stakes national curriculum testing distracted teachers from assessment as part of teaching, to assessment becoming outcome-driven.

One of Dorset's School Improvement Strategies was the establishment of a School Improvement Network Service for headteachers, subject leaders and teachers. This service offered a range of conferences and seminars. Our current Head of School Improvement – then a Primary Inspector – sought to bring the most inspirational speakers into the LEA to inspire our schools and our teachers. Amongst those speakers were Paul Black, Dylan Wiliam and Shirley Clarke, on several occasions. They inspired our headteachers and their staff to focus on assessment in classrooms, assessment as part of learning and to consider how pupils could be more actively involved in that learning.

Practice was being developed, shared and deepened as an ongoing process. Many schools were dabbling with effective assessment strategies that made a difference to pupil learning, to the self-esteem and confidence of pupils. Teachers were excited that they could see immediate impact on pupil attitudes, behaviour and enjoyment of learning.

'Assessment for Learning' became a key activity in the LEA Education Development Plan. This ensured the funding to engage in some detailed action research. We were privileged to become one of Shirley's 'Learning Teams'.

The most difficult task for me as the Assessment Inspector was to select 15 schools to form the Learning Team. Clear criteria had to be agreed and rigorously applied to the selection process. We were determined that only the keenest schools and teachers would be invited. The Learning Team included Advanced Skills Teachers, Consultant Leading Teachers within the LEA, newly qualified teachers and Headteachers. We were keen to include a range of

(continued)

different schools, from small rural Primary to large Infant and a couple of Middle schools. Two teachers from each school made a commitment to the project. The project ran from June to November 2004 over a period of four days.

Shirley launched the project with very detailed resource findings. The days were active, with teachers engaged in practical assessment strategies that they could instantly take back to their classrooms and try out. The teachers made the commitment to do the action research and be prepared to share their findings within the learning team. They responded well to the clear framework which the project demanded. Throughout the four days, teachers' confidence grew and the buzz became louder.

The whole range of formative assessment strategies was trialled. However, there was a strong emphasis among the learning team members in researching 'talking partners' and developing this approach as an improvement tool in the classroom. The impact was immediately visible. To quote one teacher from the Learning Team: *'My pupils are developing important lifelong learning skills as a result of developing the talking partners strategy.'*

The highlight of the project was the Presentation Showcase on Day 4, the final day of the project. It was fantastic to see the teachers arriving with their large white cardboard posters, reflecting the success of the formative assessment strategies from their classrooms. We had video footages, quotes from pupils, teachers and parents. It was an occasion for celebration.

The teachers presented their findings to an audience of LEA personnel, headteachers and teachers. Schools who had expressed an interest in developing formative assessment strategies as a tool for whole-school improvement were invited to this presentation. Since then, the desire to engage in high quality formative assessment in classrooms has continued to grow.

Under the umbrella of the Primary Strategy, local networks have emerged to develop work in this area. The teachers from the project are in high demand to share their practice and tell their stories.

The action research project has had huge impact on our School Improvement work in the LEA. Many teachers who were dabbling with formative strategies now see the importance of those strategies as tools for improvement in their own classrooms.

To meet the demands of our schools, we have developed a strategic LEA plan to build capacity in this crucial area of development. Through EDP funding I will lead the teachers from Shirley's project in broadening and deepening their research, continuing to share their practice and writing up accounts of that practice for dissemination to all schools and for our LEA website. These teachers will support our LEA Primary National Strategy capacity-building plan, by becoming Consultant Leading Teachers for formative assessment.

(continued)

The Primary National Strategy Networks have provided another vehicle for collaborative work in this field. Currently schools are preparing bids to secure Primary Strategy funding to develop formative assessment work as networks.

As you can see, as an LEA we plan to continue this work as part of strengthening the learning and teaching process in our schools, and to enhance the experiences and outcomes for all Dorset pupils.

Finally, I would like to leave you with some quotes from our very youngest pupils. Pupils in Year 1 in Wyke Regis Infant School were asked for their views on 'talking partners'.

This is what they had to say:

'Jonnie used his hands to show me how to build the house of sticks. It made it clearer for me.' (They had been reading *The Three Little Pigs*.)

'I liked knowing what Ben was going to do with his picture.'

'It is fun and good to hear someone else's ideas.'

'It made me change my mind.'

With thanks to Teresa Bain, Senior Inspector, Primary Assessment, Dorset LEA.

3. Key messages for teachers, heads, LEA staff and other trainers and educators

■ **Formative Assessment evolves through continual action research – it is not another initiative.**

This distinction needs to be clear at the outset of any development. Teachers need to feel empowered and confident to trial, modify, experiment and create, to feed back their successes and problems, and to be prepared to spend time discussing and analysing their findings.

■ **Senior Management Team support is essential.**

Senior managers should not only support the introduction of formative assessment, but need to be committed to seeing it happen, by giving time and resource support for extensive trialling and meetings. New policies on assessment usually need to be drawn up reflecting formative assessment principles and practice. SMT also need to ensure there are systems in place for new staff to be inducted into formative assessment.

■ It takes time.

Formative assessment often involves major change in people's thinking and needs time to be trialled, discussed and created by schools. It would be better to wait until there is a serious commitment on the school or LEA development plan to formative assessment, than to try to rush it in a few staff meetings or training days.

■ Decide the best way to start.

Feedback from schools indicates that it is more effective to ask a few keen teachers to trial some of the strategies first before embarking on whole-school trialling. These teachers not only feed back their work at a later date, but have often by then ironed out practical problems which everyone otherwise would have encountered. Most importantly, their success makes the notion of formative assessment credible and viable for the individual school context. There is often natural curiosity from others about how the action research is going, so the osmotic effect happens naturally at this stage.

What is needed is a plan, extending over at least three years, in which a few small groups are supported for a two-year exploration, and they then form a basis of experience and expertise for disseminating within the school and supporting their colleagues in making similar explorations for themselves.

(Black et al., 2002)

■ Base decisions on research principles.

The summary given at the end of each chapter lists the things that really matter. When deciding on ways of working, take account of these principles rather than the practical strategies. If the strategies are trialled without the underlying principle being understood, teachers can use them superficially. It is better to present the research in each case and first ask teachers what they believe they are already doing to fulfil those principles. The ideas in this book can then be given as some possible things to trial.

■ Build on existing practice.

Any practical strategies outlined in this book are derived from teachers, and should be seen as another suggestion *adding* to each teacher's existing repertoire, rather than replacing it.

Teachers need to be encouraged to be action researchers – trialling not only ideas from this book, but their own ideas. There will be successes and failures, and children and staff need time to grow into new ways of working and thinking, so they need to be encouraged not to give up! The end result should be modified strategies, which schools and teachers have created for themselves, using books like this, and others referenced here, as a resource.

■ Keep a journal.

It is a good idea to encourage teachers to keep a 'learning journal' in which they jot their ideas, make notes on successful lessons, record quotes from children and so on. This keeps the focus on formative assessment and equips teachers with specific anecdotes for departmental or other staff meetings. Too often, teachers forget the details of spectacular lessons and can only speak in generalities. The specifics allow other teachers to see clearly what happened and how it impacted on child learning, making their own application more feasible.

■ Don't go it alone.

Get teachers to observe each other and work closely together wherever possible. Observing each other teach, with a clear focus, is highly productive if there is mutual trust and respect.

Try to get involved in a learning network community group or create a network of schools in which the same element is being explored, so that teachers can be observed and strategies and findings can be shared. Visit my website (www.shirleyclarke-education.org) for regular updates on the findings of the various Learning Teams around the country.

■ Involve the children.

Ask children for their opinions about the strategies throughout. Ask for their feelings about particular elements before and then after introducing formative assessment. This will obviously become more fruitful as time progresses and children have had more opportunities to discuss and analyse together and put forward their views more freely.

Creating a School Council is a further indicator to children that they have a say in their education and that their opinions are valued. Children in one school put forward the request that they would like all teachers to know which strategies used across the school by the various teachers were considered most successful in helping them learn. The school was well into formative assessment practices, so it is not surprising that such a confident request was made. Formative assessment allows children to communicate their needs with confidence.

■ Keep it going.

Once formative assessment has been introduced, it is important to keep momentum in the following ways:

- Make sure the strategies are monitored, especially by classroom observation.

- Make sure the strategies are visually obvious throughout the school.

- Refer to the strategies during whole-school events such as assemblies, so that all staff and children know the common language of achievement.

- Write an assessment policy which outlines exactly how formative assessment is carried out.

- Produce parent-friendly news-sheets along the way so that parents are fully informed and encouraged to support their child's new development.

- Produce summaries of the assessment policy when it is finished, to show all relevant parties.

- Continue to review the strategies in action, consulting all parties involved – especially children.

Endnote from Shirley

Teachers are rarely told how expert they have become. In my travels around the world I have been struck many times by how far we have come in the last 15 years. UK teachers have exceptional expertise, which is still developing and growing, in their own subjects and in basing learning on learning objectives. They have access to wonderful resources and have considerably elevated their expectations of children.

Feedback from teachers applying formative assessment strategies has been overwhelming. As the research demonstrates, formative assessment makes a significant difference to children's progress – in their ability to be confident, critical learners, to achieve more than ever before and in raising their self-esteem.

What is needed now is high teacher morale, greater power and more professional confidence. The ingredients are all there for teachers to pay more attention to *learning* than coverage, to focusing on what works best for the learning rather than for accountability, and to make lessons fit the *children's* learning needs rather than the needs of outside parties. Hopefully, this book will inspire teachers to grab their professional confidence with both hands.

Endnote from OFSTED (at Roman Road Primary School – Gateshead Learning Team)

> *Pupils' involvement in evaluating their own work is promoted strongly and very effectively in lessons. Teachers throughout the school plan well, question pupils well, manage them effectively and encourage them to work hard to develop their understanding.*

Endnote from teachers

> *This is the best thing I've done in all my teaching career!*

> *It's been good because there's no pressure. It's about trying ideas, discussing them and adapting. It's really successful!*

> *Previously there was so much to do and to cover. Now there's a move towards learning skills with knowledge and understanding.*

> *Formative assessment encourages all children of any ability to access tasks and allows them to take responsibility for their own learning. It enables them to improve their own work and boosts self-esteem.*

Endnote from children at Roman Road School

> *I like formative assessment because you learn from your mistakes and constantly get better. You can also show off your improved work.*

> *I like formative assessment because you can't be perfect first time so it gives you time to be the best you can be.*

> *Formative assessment helps you feel good about yourself.*

References

Assessment Reform Group (2002) *Assessment for Learning: Ten Principles* (www.assessment-reform-group.org.uk)

Black, P. and Wiliam, D. (1998) *Inside the Black Box: Raising Standards through Classroom Assessment*, London: King's College School of Education.

Black, P., Harrison, C., Lee, C., Marshall, B. and Wiliam, D. (2003) *Assessment for Learning*, Open University Press.

Butler, R. (1988) 'Enhancing and undermining intrinsic motivation; the effects of task-involving and ego-involving evaluation on interest and performance', *British Journal of Educational Psychology, 58*, 1–14.

Clarke, S. (2001) *Unlocking Formative Assessment*, Hodder and Stoughton.

Clarke, S. (2003) *Enriching Feedback in the Primary Classroom*, Hodder and Stoughton.

Clarke, S. website for previous publications and Learning Teams updates: www.shirleyclarke-education.org

Crooks, T. (2001) Paper prepared for the 2001 Annual Meeting of the British Educational Research Association (BERA), Leeds, England, 13–15 September 2001 (in proceedings, but not presented because of travel delays caused by terrorist actions).

De Bono, E., in O'Sullivan (2003) *Questions Worth Asking*, The Brighton and Hove Assessment for Learning Project, Brighton and Hove LEA.

DfES *Speaking, Listening, Learning: working with children in Key Stages 1 and 2:* www.dfes.gov.uk

Dweck, C. (1986) 'Motivational processes affecting learning', *American Psychologist, 41*, 1041–8.

Eppig, P. (1981) *Education by Design* – used in the UK as Critical Skills program by Success@Bristol (Bristol Education Action Zone).

Hall, K. and Burke, W. (2003) Making Formative Assessment Work, Open University Press.

Kent County Council: *Open Questions to Develop Thinking across the Foundation Stage and Key Stage 1 Curriculum* (contact Lesley Allum 01732 525000 or Judy Venner 01227 772992).

Kluger, A. N. and DeNisi, A. (1996) 'The effects of feedback interventions on performance: a historical review, a meta-analysis, and a preliminary feedback intervention theory', *Psychological Bulletin*, *119*, 2, 258–84.

O'Sullivan, C. (2003) *Questions Worth Asking*, The Brighton and Hove LEA Assessment for Learning Project.

Perrenoud, P. (1991) 'Towards a pragmatic approach to formative evaluation', in Weston, P. (ed.) *Assessment of Pupils' Achievement: Motivation and School Success*, Amsterdam: Swets and Zeitlinger.

QCA website: www.qca.org.uk for the Assessment for Learning site.

Rowe, M. B. (1974) 'Relation of wait-time and rewards to the development of language, logic and fate control', *Journal of Research in Science Teaching*, *11*, 4, 292 (in *High Scope*, 1995).

Sadler, R. (1989) 'Formative assessment and the design of instructional systems', *Instructional Science*, *18*, 119–44.

Suffolk LEA references: www.slamnet.org.uk

Thinkabouts by Alan Peat and Barry Silsby: www.alanpeat.com